MISADVENTURES

IN THE

ENGLISH LANGUAGE

By the same author:

I Used to Know That
My Grammar and I (or should that be 'Me'?)
A Classical Education
An Apple a Day
Answers to Rhetorical Questions
Pushing the Envelope
The I Used to Know That Activity Book
Back to Basics
Kicking the Bucket at the Drop of a Hat
500 Words You Should Know
New Words for Old

MISADVENTURES
IN THE
ENGLISH LANGUAGE

CAROLINE
TAGGART

Michael O'Mara Books Limited

First published in Great Britain in 2016 by
Michael O'Mara Books Limited
9 Lion Yard
Tremadoc Road
London SW4 7NQ

A CIP catalogue record for this book is available from the British Library.

Papers used by Michael O'Mara Books Limited are natural, recyclable products made from wood grown in sustainable forests. The manufacturing processes conform to the environmental regulations of the country of origin.

ISBN: 978-1-78243-647-8 in hardback print format
ISBN: 978-1-78243-649-2 in ebook format

1 3 5 7 9 10 8 6 4 2

Designed and typeset by K.DESIGN, Winscombe, Somerset

Printed and bound by CPI Group (UK) Ltd, Croydon, CR0 4YY

www.mombooks.com

Contents

Introduction

Last Christmas my sister gave me a mug that said, 'I am silently correcting your grammar.' She thought, for some reason, that it might amuse my friends – several of whom have since spluttered with laughter and assured me she was right.

About the same time I was staying with a friend who had recently joined a cycling group. In the course of conversation she remarked that she really enjoyed it because everyone was so unjudgemental. 'That's an interesting word,' I said. 'Do you have many judgemental friends?'

'Oh God,' she replied. 'I forgot I was talking to *you*.'

At that moment we were interrupted, so I'll probably never know what she did mean, but these two incidents sum up much of what this book is about. I wince (I hope silently) when people say, 'Between you and I' or 'work colleagues'; I was intrigued and a little concerned when a friend described her two children as 'literally chalk and cheese'; and I do listen closely (obsessively?) to people's choice of words. I've also, because of books I have written over the last few years, had lots of opportunity to consider and pontificate on issues of language, the 'rights' and the 'wrongs', and to form opinions on what matters and what – IMHO – doesn't.

Since the arrival of email, texts and social media, there has been more discussion than ever before about the English language and whether or not it is going to the dogs. But disgust at recent changes and at the ignorance of youth is far from being a twenty-first-century innovation. Consider this heartfelt complaint, from Charles Eliot, President of Harvard:

Bad spelling, incorrectness as well as inelegance of expression in writing, ignorance of the simplest rules of punctuation ... are far from rare among young men of 18 otherwise well prepared for college studies.

It was written in 1871 and surely the only clue that it wasn't written yesterday is the assumption that all students are male.

Those who are resistant to change hark back to rules that others consider archaic or maintain were never appropriate in the first place. Those who find this attitude pretentious insist that, if everyone says it or writes it, it can't be wrong. Rule-lovers sometimes counter with, 'It may be common, but that doesn't stop it being (with a pause and a shudder) *common*.' Snobbery has always had, and probably always will have, a role to play in what we consider 'right' and 'wrong' in language. This book will look at that aspect too.

My attitude – and that's all it is, a personal attitude – falls somewhere in the middle of all this. I believe in precise language, the right word in the right place. I think it's a shame to lose nuances (such as the much argued-over difference between *uninterested* and *disinterested*) for want of paying a little attention. I admire elegant language, beautiful language – subjective terms, obviously, but it is hard to beat the frisson of recognition that you feel (okay, that *I* feel) when a good writer puts an idea you have always had into words you suddenly wish you had chosen. On a less highfalutin plane, I think – indeed, I'll stick my neck out here and say I know – that punctuation is there to help convey meaning; so is correct spelling. Obeying grammatical rules can help avoid ambiguity – if you say what you mean, you don't have to shrug and say, 'Well, you know what I mean.'

On the other hand, language, usage, vocabulary change all the time and something that was correct a hundred years ago may seem laughably stilted now, just as a word that early twentieth-century pedants abhorred may have become commonplace. So in the course of this book I'll be explaining some of the rules, giving examples of where they actually do matter and trying to be neither too pedantic nor too laissez-faire. I'll try to help in areas that I know some people find difficult; I'll be celebrating inventiveness and denouncing clichés and jargon; and I'll have the occasional rant about things that just happen to annoy me. Also, because misadventures don't have to be catastrophic and because language is one of the great loves of my life, I'll be trying to have some fun and impart some of my enthusiasm along the way.

Before we go any further: a glossary

There's no avoiding a few technical terms in a book like this. Some of them are defined in the text itself, but I felt the most important deserved a special mention up front. Please, if you are confident that you know the difference between an adjective and an adverb, a clause and a phrase, feel free to turn the page and get on with the more exciting stuff, or go and have a cup of tea while the rest of us get this out of the way.

Parts of speech

These are the categories into which words are divided according to their function in a sentence.

A *noun* names a thing, person, place, concept: *apple, Isaac Newton, England, gravity.*

A *pronoun* stands in place of a noun: *I*, *me*, *you*, *he*, *she*, *him*, *her* and so on.

An *adjective* describes or modifies a noun or pronoun: the *wicked* uncle, she looks *tired*.

A *verb* is a 'doing' word: it tells you what is happening, and when (or indeed if) it happened. A *finite verb* coupled with a noun or pronoun also specifies number – singular or plural – and person (see opposite). It may consist of one word (she *came* home on the bus) or several (she *could have come* in a taxi) and it's an essential part of a grammatical sentence – a sentence isn't a sentence without one. Non-finite verbs serve various other purposes and are either infinitives (*to come*, *to go*, *to faff about*), present participles (*coming*, *going*, *faffing*) or past participles (*came*, *gone*, *faffed*).

An *adverb* modifies a verb, an adjective or another adverb: he walked *slowly*; we took a *very* scenic route; I drove *extremely* cautiously. More about adverbs on page 72.

A *preposition* is one of those little words such as *to*, *at*, *up*, *down*, *over*, *under*, that show where one thing is in relation to another.

A *conjunction* joins two words or two parts of a sentence: strawberries *and* cream; generous *but* not extravagant; he seems happy, *yet* sometimes I catch him looking wistful.

An *interjection* is something like *Stop! Help! Alas!* that shows emotion or reaction. It isn't grammatically part of a sentence – it's what is called a sentence fragment and stands on its own (often followed by an exclamation mark).

A *determiner* determines or limits the meaning of a

noun or noun phrase. The most common determiners are *the*, *a* and *an*, but this category also includes *this*, *that*, *these*, *those*; quantifiers such as *some*, *many* and *few* (which give an indication of quantity or number) and the possessive adjectives, *my*, *your*, *his*, *her*, *its*, *our*, *their*. A determiner identifies *this* programme as opposed to *that* one, for example, or *my* house as opposed to *your* house.

Person

In grammatical terms, a person is defined as 'a category into which pronouns and forms of verb are divided depending on whether they refer to the speaker, the person addressed or some other individual, thing, etc.' In other words, the first person is *I* or *we*; the second person is *you*; and the third person is everything else – *he*, *she*, *it* or *they*.

Subject, verb, object

At its most basic, a sentence consists of a subject, a verb and an object: the subject does something, the verb tells you what that something is, and the object is the thing it is done to.

I (subject) *ate* (verb) *an apple* (object).
Clare (subject) *will bring* (verb) *pudding* (object).
Luke (subject) *is driving* (verb) *his parents* (object).

These are all *direct objects.* Some verbs also take an *indirect object* – see pages 70–1.

Clauses and phrases

The difference between a clause and a phrase is that a clause contains a subject and a finite verb, though it may not make a complete sentence.

I ate an apple is a clause; if you put a full stop at the end and leave it at that, it's also a sentence.

I ate an apple that was beginning to go brown is a sentence that consists of two clauses: *I ate an apple* is the *main clause* and can stand on its own; *that was beginning to go brown* is a *subsidiary clause.* It contains a finite verb (*was beginning*) but isn't a complete sentence.

A phrase is a word or group of words that contributes to a clause, and it may take various forms. A *verb phrase* contains a verb and possibly an object, but not a subject, so *ate an apple* and *was beginning to go brown* are both verb phrases. A *noun phrase* serves the purpose of a noun: *an apple*, for example. But it can be more complicated than that: in the sentence *the author had written* **twenty historical romances** *set in pre-revolutionary France*, the words in bold are all part of a noun phrase. You can have *adjectival phrases* and *adverbial phrases*, *prepositional phrases* and *participial phrases* – we'll deal with them as and when they crop up.

CHAPTER 1

How very dare you?

Moving with the times

It's absurd to suggest that language doesn't and shouldn't change. Take the title I've given to this chapter. Not so long ago I heard a television interviewer ask this question, expressing mock outrage at something her interviewee had said. The expression was new to me: I subsequently discovered it had been a catchphrase ten years ago on a television comedy I hadn't seen. I then checked through the Oxford English Dictionary online's entry for *very* – some 10,000 words, perhaps eighty headings and subheadings and over 400 quotations – and there is not one example of its being used in this way. Not the remotest grammatical or historical justification for it. But in the real world that doesn't matter two hoots: if enough of the three million people who had watched the original programme picked it up, it could become part of the language.

That use of *very* could even be adapted into other expressions. *Why very must you do that*? might suggest that I had asked you a hundred times not to; *where very have I left the car keys* could be a politer way of wondering what the hell I have done with them. There's no evidence that this is happening: my point is that it *could* happen, if enough people wanted it to. It's not far removed from the use of *so* in expressions such as *That is so not going to happen* or *You are so going to die if you do that again*, which the OED describes as 'forming nonstandard grammatical constructions'. Nonstandard maybe, but widely used, widely understood and probably here to stay.

Then there's *like*, as in *You are, like, so going to die if you do that again* or, less explicitly, *And I'm like ...* (accompanied by an annoyed, impatient or baffled facial expression but no further words). That is, like, so nonstandard.

In another borrowing from a television series, a friend described an outing that hadn't gone according to plan as an 'omnishambles'. Coined in 2012 for the BBC series *The Thick of It* (which morphed into *Veep* in the US and inspired the movie *In the Loop*), *omnishambles* became the OED's word of the year in 2013, entered the dictionaries, and left our vocabulary richer. It means, as I'm sure you know, a cock-up (or any other expression you choose that ends in -*up*) of spectacular proportions, but is *so* much more expressive.

A catchphrase passes into the language because we like it and it serves a purpose. Then it may stay forever or hang around for a while before drifting off again

(I don't know anyone who still says, 'Ooh, you are awful, but I like you' or 'Well isn't that special?'). But there's a lot more to language change than catchphrases. New words have been coined – or existing ones used in new ways – since time immemorial, particularly by journalists, showmen and others who want to grab the public's attention. It doesn't matter if the term catches on or disappears without trace, as long as it has stayed around long enough to make people dip their hands in their pockets and buy a newspaper or a ticket. William Cooke's Famous Equestrian Circus, visiting Brighton in the 1850s, billed itself as 'hippo-dramatic', secure in the knowledge that a substantial part of its audience would know that *hippo* came from the Greek for *horse* and wouldn't turn up expecting to see animals that were squatter, heavier and more cumbersome. The word presumably fell out of use when Greek became less familiar, circuses boasted other attractions and people demanded their money back because there were no hippos.

Where do we find them?

New words – also known as neologisms – can be divided into at least four categories:

1)   New coinages to cover new inventions, discoveries

or developments: *amphetamine*, *anti-oxidant*, *television*, *testosterone*.

2) Coinages formed from amalgamating two or more existing words, again to deal with a new need: *blog*, *brunch*, *motel*, *workaholic*.

3) Words adopted from other languages, often to accompany foodstuffs, utensils, fabrics, fashions and building styles that we have discovered on our travels: *chutney*, *spaghetti*, *sushi*, *tandoori*, *wok*, *batik*, *sari*, *bungalow*.

4) Existing words whose meanings are adapted or added to in order to cope with new phenomena: *avatar*, *disc*, *file*, *forum*, *satellite*.

In this last category, old meanings aren't necessarily abandoned: an *avatar* is still a manifestation of a Hindu god, despite also being a graphic representation of the user within a computer game; and you can still find *discs* made of cartilage between the vertebrae of your spine, even though they now also come in vinyl, compact or digital-video formats.

This sort of change can be tricky if the new meaning is an unpleasant one. Harmless people working in stables or harmless men about to be married may want to find another name for themselves since internet *grooming* has become the problem that it is. It may be a comfort to those harmless grooms to know that the perpetrators of internet grooming are usually called *groomers* – although this won't be much consolation to those other innocent souls who offer grooming services for domestic pets. The internet *troll* is another nasty new phenomenon, but at least the characters in Scandinavian fairy tales after whom they are named were disagreeable in the first place.

If we go back in time a little, we realize that adapting meanings was happening long before the technological revolution. In about 1940, F. Scott Fitzgerald put 'freelance' – a word I have been using without giving it a thought since I became one a quarter of a century ago – in inverted commas, suggesting it was a new usage. *Freelance* used to mean a military mercenary, a 'free lance' who owed no particular allegiance to anyone but offered his services (and presumably his lance) for a fee to anyone who needed them. When Fitzgerald used it to refer to a Hollywood scriptwriter who worked not under contract but for any studio that had temporary need of his services, he was – just like those who altered the meaning of *avatar* and *troll* – giving a newish twist to an established word.

I read recently that someone most Brits would consider a 'national treasure' disliked the term. Curiosity sparked, I discovered that it originally meant something more literal: 'the accumulated wealth of a nation' and thence 'an artefact, place or phenomenon thought in some way to embody or contribute to a nation's cultural heritage or identity'. The Brazilian footballer Pelé was officially designated a 'national treasure' in the early 1960s to stop foreign clubs luring him away, but it seems to be only in the twenty-first century that we began to toss the term around in the UK to describe actors, writers and TV personalities from Dame Judi Dench to the rather younger Stephen Fry, and in the USA elderly actors such as former 'Golden Girl' Betty White. The OED defines this particular kind of national treasure as 'a public figure whose reputation and renown afford similarly emblematic status', but it's really not much more than 'someone who's been around for a long time and whom we all admire'. That's a long way from 'the sum of assets owned or controlled by the state' that William Pitt the Elder meant when he used the phrase in the House of Commons in 1766.

It's interesting, too, to consider the way words become unacceptable. Slang or informal terms for members of various races, religious and sexual orientations come in and out of taboo, or are permissible only among insiders (a Jew, for example, seems to be allowed to insult a fellow Jew in a way that would be totally inappropriate coming from anyone else). The way we talk about women has evolved, too. A venerable golf club in Scotland was recently in the news for refusing to open its membership to what it called 'ladies'. Amid much uproar, one journalist wrote that 'it is only old sexists and over-enthusiastic Zumba teachers who use the word now'. I beg to differ: I've heard enthusiastic Pilates teachers use it too. But it is a very long time since I have been asked in a pub – as I routinely was as a student – whether the half a lager I was buying was 'for a lady'.[1]

The colour of your money

Throughout history we've used 'black' to convey something wicked, threatening or anti-establishment: *the Black Death, black magic, Black Sabbath. Black Monday* (or Wednesday or whatever) has been used to refer to stock-market crashes, massive power cuts or riots with high death tolls. But in the last few years the UK has adopted the Americanism *Black Friday* for the day after Thanksgiving, when Christmas shopping begins, special offers are made and lots of money is spent. It's the day when companies, however bad the year has been, start making a profit. They go *into the black* – a good thing, dating from the days when accounts clerks wrote positive numbers (income) in black ink and negative numbers (expenses) in red.

---

1 For the benefit of the young: if I had said yes, the lager would have been served in a 'lady's glass', one of those shapely ones without a handle. A man ordering half a lager was given a jug: the old-fashioned design of beer glass, with dimples and a handle. Amazing, eh? But absolutely commonplace, I assure you, in the 1970s.

What I want to know is: if we take this approach to the word *black*, what are we going to do next time the world's stock markets crash? Call it Maroon Monday? Turquoise Tuesday? Fawn Friday? They really don't have the same ring.

I read the news today . . .

Terms relating to current events come and go in much the same way as catchphrases. From McCarthyism to Beatlemania, many of them have served their purpose, then entered history with no value except their original one. But the Western world's greatest political scandal happened to be born in an office complex in Washington DC called Watergate, where the Democratic National Committee based itself in preparation for the 1972 US presidential election. The second part of that name – conveniently a 'real' word – has lent itself to unnumbered scandals since, from Irangate, when the US administration was involved in selling arms to Iran, to Plebgate, when a British MP allegedly addressed a policeman in Downing Street as a pleb. It was also gleefully pointed out that this bad-tempered encounter took place in a gateway, allowing those who so desired to refer to it as Gategate. This is a fine example of the randomness of it all: if, in 1972, the Democratic National Committee had chosen to base itself in the Hilton or the Sheraton, these words couldn't have arisen.

Loanation flourished briefly in 2006 in connection with a UK political scandal – a cross between a *loan* and a *donation*, it was the sort of loan that didn't have to be repaid. Unless a similar scandal rears its head in the future, it's another word that will have had its fifteen minutes of fame and then disappeared.

Another candidate for 'flash in the pan' status is *Smombies* – the 'Smartphone zombies' who are always walking into things, people and (apparently) a 6 metre-tall sculpture on the green outside Salisbury Cathedral because they are paying so much attention to their phones that they are oblivious to the world around them. Destined to be short-lived, I suggest, because *Smombies* will surely, over a generation or two, all be run over and wiped out.

There are lots of words in popular use at the moment that weren't around a generation ago. Only time will tell if they make it:

- *Futureproofing* – preparing yourself for a foreseeable future, such as building an extension to your house so that you won't have to move when the children are bigger.

- *Kidult* – an adult who is interested in entertainment such as computer games aimed primarily at children. Also *adultescent*. In these days of constant reassessment of family and gender roles, it's hardly surprising to come across *sharents* – *parents* who *share* domestic and child-caring tasks – but this term is also applied to those who *over-share*, by persistently posting on Facebook boastful remarks about their offspring's achievements and other aspects of their often very dull lives. It's a depressing sign of the times: this sort of bragging used to be confined to Christmas round-robin letters. Now we're subjected to it all year round.

- *Me-mail* – carefully targeted marketing email, the sort of thing marketeers believe *I* will respond to because it is relevant to *me*.

- *Millennials* – those reaching adulthood around the year 2000. At the time of writing, this is marketing speak for *twenty-* or *thirty-somethings*, but it's a term that could easily come to replace *baby boomers* (those born in large numbers either immediately after the Second World War or in the 1960s) to denote people of a certain age whose spending habits follow a predictable pattern.

- *Pescetarian* or *pescatarian* – a vegetarian who eats fish (*demi-veg* is an alternative, though some would make the distinction that a *demi-veg* will also eat chicken). I've also come across *pesco-vegetarian*, meaning the same thing, but surely this is both too long and too pretentious to last.

And so on.

Word-creation schemes

You don't have to be on television or in the news to come up with new words and expressions. There are all sorts of other ways. Deriving *burgle* from the much older *burglar* (what is known as a *back-formation*) was originally done for comic effect: *The burglar who attempted to enter that room would never burgle again*, wrote the now largely forgotten novelist Mortimer Collins in 1872. There was a fearsome tawny mastiff named Lion roaming the room in question, intimidating enough to make any burglar rethink his chosen career path. This line must at the time have been as witty as P. G. Wodehouse's famous *I could see that, if not actually disgruntled, he was far from being gruntled*, written some sixty years later.

Oddly, *to burgle* has become an everyday, non-jocular word, while *gruntled* is still used only in frivolous contexts. But give it another half-century or so and who knows? People once shuddered at the use of *burgle* (presumably they insisted on *to commit a burglary*); now they tend to save their disapproval for *burglarize*, although this has a long-standing pedigree in the US and was used by the exaggeratedly well-spoken – and certainly not American – Sydney Greenstreet character in *The Maltese Falcon* in 1941.

Those who don't approve of social media should be careful not to be too critical of the verb *to trend*. The OED has acknowledged it since 2015 in the sense of 'to generate a large amount of social media activity over a short time span; to become popular or prevalent on social media networks'. But it existed a thousand years ago in various senses to do with turning round or veering off in another direction: in fact, it's a good six centuries older than any meaning of *trend* as a noun; and eight centuries older than the figurative 'general course, tendency or drift of action or thought' which gave rise to the modern concept of *trending*.

The passage of time frequently makes the outrageous less outrageous (although I don't think it yet makes it *rageous* or *inrageous*). Certainly it makes the foreign less foreign. Reading a popular detective story first published in 1940, I came across, in the space of five pages, *delicatessen*, *personnel* and *nil*, all printed in italics, acknowledging that they were borrowings from other languages (German, French and Latin respectively, as it happens). Who, writing such a novel today, would consider for one moment that these words were foreign – and how many people under the age of forty, when expressing indifference to something, would say that their interest in it was *nil* rather than *zero* (a word we borrowed from the French in the seventeenth century and whose origins can be traced back to Arabic)?

In another detective story from the 1930s (those British Library reissues have a lot to answer for), a lad of twenty-something, making a deal with his father, ends his proposition with 'Okay?' 'Okay,' replies the father. 'If you must use such a vulgar expression.' Later in the book, when the son says, 'Oke', the father replies, 'Please . . . not oke. Okay, if you really must give way to these vulgar Americanisms. But not oke.' You wonder what he might have made of *okey-dokey*, a variant that came into use about the same time.

Bend it like Tesco

As I was writing this there came an announcement that a well-known UK supermarket was going to stop selling the traditionally shaped croissant, on the basis that customers find it easier to spread butter and jam on a straighter version. The *Guardian* report of this news item (18 February 2016, although I did check the date to make sure it wasn't 1 April) didn't say this in so many words. It said – and really you couldn't make this up – that customers preferred the straighter version because of its 'optimized "spreadability factor"'.

This clearly ignores the fact that *croissant* is the French word for *crescent* (indeed, in the USA *croissants* are sometimes called *crescent rolls*), that the pastry was given that name *because* of its shape and that, therefore, if it isn't crescent-shaped it isn't a croissant. The supermarket in question is a powerful one in the UK; if its straight croissants become popular enough, the word will change its meaning, however much Francophones may laugh.

Rebecca Gowers in an engrossing book called *Horrible Words* mentions that there was a time when *reliable*, *knowledgeable* and *laughable* all offended one self-styled expert or another. Shakespeare and Dryden both used *laughable* to mean funny, able to be laughed at; when Thomas Carlyle used it in the mid-nineteenth century he meant what we would mean today – absurd, ludicrous. Creative writers are always looking for innovative ways to express things: that nuance, that use of a word in an unusual context, that completely new coinage may be eye-catching, exhilarating, thought-provoking. It may give readers or theatregoers an insight they have never had before. If it is picked up by the masses and enters everyday English, the writer has to come up with something else to achieve the same effect next time. And so it goes on, with the language stretching out its tentacles in all sorts of different directions. If you don't believe me, Google it, to drag in another verb that didn't exist thirty years ago.

One final example of the joy to be found in inventing new words. Bill Bryson in *The Road to Little Dribbling* mentions a brand of shirts called Seidensticker Splendesto. He decides that *splendesto* ought to be 'a word in its own right, denoting a higher level of excellence beyond splendid. I even thought of a slogan for them: "Splendesto – when splendid isn't good enough". He is, as he so often is, absolutely right. *Please* let this catch on.

CHAPTER 2

Finger's crossed

Punctuation and why it – usually – matters

The eighteenth-century landscape architect 'Capability' Brown, showing an acquaintance round the gardens he had created at Hampton Court, pointed out, 'There, I make a comma, and there, where a more decided turn is proper, I make a colon; at another part, where an interruption is desirable to break the view, a parenthesis; now a full stop, and then I begin another subject.' It's reasonable to assume that Brown's companion knew what he was talking about, and surely not wildly over-optimistic to believe that this analogy helped him to appreciate the subtleties of the garden. I'm hoping, 300 years on, that it might help you to appreciate some of the subtleties of punctuation. It even has a couple of semicolons in it for good measure.

Punctuation may be the bane of many people's lives, but its intentions are entirely honourable: it's there to help. It should – it really should – clarify meaning, indicate emphasis, distinguish a statement from a question or an exclamation and show where one train of thought stops and another begins.

Commas

The comma – that little pause that is less substantial than a full stop, a colon or a semicolon – is the most versatile piece of punctuation we have. These are just a handful of the many purposes it can serve:

- **It separates items in a list**:

  There was an array of sandwiches on offer: ham, cheese, tuna mayonnaise and egg.

It comes in handy when one of the items contains *and*: if the array of sandwiches includes *ham, cheese, tuna mayonnaise, and egg and cress,* the comma after *mayonnaise* should prevent anyone from ordering *tuna mayonnaise and egg* – or indeed *tuna mayonnaise, egg and cress* – in the mistaken belief that these combinations are on the menu.

- It comes **after the name of a speaker to introduce a piece of direct speech**, or before and after the name of a speaker if it falls in the middle of a speech:

  Paul said, 'I suppose you're right and I apologize.'
  'I suppose you're right,' said Paul, 'and I apologize.'

If what Paul had said had been two separate sentences, we would still have had the comma after the first one, but a full stop after his name.

> *Paul said, 'I suppose you're right. I won't do it again.'*
> *'I suppose you're right,' said Paul. 'I won't do it again.'*

- It **separates an introductory word, phrase or clause** from the rest of the sentence:

> *Yes, I'd love to come.*
> *After all, tomorrow is another day.*
> *Whenever the sun comes out, everyone seems more cheerful.*

- It **separates one phrase or clause from another** within a sentence:

> *He hadn't expected her to come, but there she was, standing by the gate, looking impatiently at her watch.*

- A pair of commas act as a **parenthesis to separate a noun or noun phrase *in apposition*** (one used to explain or expand on the noun it qualifies) from the rest of the sentence:

> *Charlotte Brontë, the eldest of the writing sisters, was the only one to marry.*
> *Mr Sinclair, the town councillor and the owner of Chester Hall, stood up to speak.*

FAQ – What's a noun in apposition, when it's at home?

Apposition is 'the placing of a word or phrase next to another, in order to qualify or explain the first'. It's a fancy way of expressing a simple concept: in the name *Ivan the Terrible*, 'the Terrible' is in apposition to 'Ivan' – it tells us which Ivan we are talking about and gives us some information about him. If you aren't hot on Russian history, *Buffy the Vampire Slayer* is the same construction. Other examples might be:

John le Carré, the best-selling author
Albert Einstein, the famous physicist
Lima, the capital of Peru

Apposition doesn't haven't to involve a name; it also occurs in:

The schoolhouse, the largest building in town
Lemon meringue pie, my favourite pudding

If any of these expressions occurred in a complete sentence, you would use a second comma:

John le Carré, the bestselling author, was interviewed on the radio.

Dad made lemon meringue pie, my favourite pudding, when I passed my exams.

Note that if you omit the bit between the commas, you are left with something that makes sense:

> *Charlotte Brontë was the only one to marry.*
> *Mr Sinclair stood up to speak.*

You can, if you wish, replace a pair of commas like this with either brackets or dashes:

> *Charlotte Brontë (the eldest of the writing sisters) was the only one to marry.*
> *Charlotte Brontë – the eldest of the writing sisters – was the only one to marry.*

It's a matter of taste and style: they all mean the same thing. But if you go for either of these options, you don't need commas. *Charlotte Brontë (the eldest of the writing sisters), was also the only one to marry* is wrong.

I recently read something about the architect Frank Lloyd Wright that began *Frank Lloyd Wright (1869– 1959), was his own greatest admirer.* It's a great line, but a poor use of a comma. If in doubt about whether or not to use a comma in circumstances like these, take out the parentheses and the bit they enclose and see what you're left with: to have a comma in *Charlotte Brontë, was the only one to marry* or *Frank Lloyd Wright, was his own greatest admirer* would just be weird.

Now let's look at the Mr Sinclair example in more detail to demonstrate the power of the comma:

In *Mr Sinclair, the town councillor and the owner of Chester Hall, stood up to speak*, the commas act as a parenthesis round the words between them: they tell us that Mr Sinclair is both the town councillor and the owner of Chester Hall.

If we take out the second comma, we are left with a list. *Mr Sinclair, the town councillor and the owner of Chester Hall stood up to speak* tells us that there were three speakers: a town councillor, the owner of Chester Hall (two different people, neither of them named) and someone called Mr Sinclair, about whom we have no other information.

Insert the second comma in a different position and you change the meaning again: *Mr Sinclair, the town councillor, and the owner of Chester Hall stood up to speak* indicates that Mr Sinclair is the town councillor but *not* the owner of Chester Hall. Again, the commas surround a piece of information that could be lifted out and leave something that makes sense: *Mr Sinclair and the owner of Chester Hall stood up to speak.*

● A pair of commas – known as bracketing commas – also acts as a **parenthesis around a part of a sentence that is grammatically independent** of the rest (again, the test is to take out the words between the commas and see if the sentence still 'works'):

> *The only possibility, it seems to me, is to pay the fine and park in the proper place next time.*

> *Bermuda, despite its reputation for hurricanes, is a lovely place for a holiday.*

Using a single comma here would be wrong: having begun your 'by the way' observation, you need to show where it finishes.

In this context, too, a pair of commas can change the meaning:

> *The leopard, which lives in the zoo, is fed twice a day* tells us there is only one leopard – it lives in the zoo and is fed twice a day.

> *The leopard which lives in the zoo is fed twice a day* suggests that there may be other leopards, roaming the streets and eating at unspecified intervals.

Restrictive practices

That example about the leopard leads us neatly into the subject of restrictive and non-restrictive clauses, also called defining and non-defining.

The difference between them is that a restrictive clause is essential to the sentence: without it, the sentence may make grammatical sense, but won't convey all the information you want. A non-restrictive clause isn't essential – it gives *extra* information.

In the leopard example, *which lives in the zoo* is non-restrictive in the first version and restrictive in the second. The first assumes that we already know about the leopard and adds the information that it lives in the zoo as a passing observation. In the second, commaless version, *which lives in the zoo* is restrictive, defining – without it we won't know which leopard is under discussion.

To give another example, consider:

The book which Ali had given me didn't interest me at all.

Which Ali had given me is defining – without it, the sentence is vague. If we say merely *The book didn't interest me at all*, we are left wondering, which book? Who cares? Or, as we will see in a later chapter, AYTMTB? On the other hand, in

The book, which Ali had given me, didn't interest me at all

the bit between commas is incidental, non-restrictive, another piece of 'by the way' information. This assumes that the book has already been mentioned and that the key point is your lack of interest in it. Its provenance is of less importance.

Read these sentences aloud, pause briefly where you see a comma, and I promise you the distinction will become clear.

Examples such as these raise another point that can be tricky: when to introduce a clause with *that* and when to use *which*. I've chosen to put *which* in all the above examples to emphasize the power of the comma, but with restrictive clauses there are options. Non-restrictive clauses are always introduced by a comma followed by *which* (or by *who* or *whom* if they refer to a person). Restrictive clauses may be introduced by *that* or *which* – or you can leave these words out altogether: *the book which Ali had given me*, *the book that Ali had given me* and *the book Ali had given me* are all grammatically correct and mean the same thing. Some people express a preference for *that* in restrictive clauses, but it's rather nice to have an occasion on which you can't go wrong.

The state of play

As a final example of how helpful a mere comma can be, here's a line from a novel in which the narrator's lover has just died. 'I was in a state of course,' she confesses. I hesitated, re-read and was briefly baffled. The novel's author was Australian – was this a local idiom with which I wasn't familiar? Was it somehow related to *a state of grace* or *a state of nerves*? Of course not, as I realized before too long. All she meant was, 'I was in a state, of course.' But the omission of the comma created something very odd.

Full stops, colons and semicolons

All of these indicate more substantial pauses than a comma, but serve different functions. You put a full stop when you have come to the end of a sentence and want to start a new thought.

She stood up and went to the window. The view was extraordinary.

If you have more complicated things to say, you may find the occasional comma creeping in:

By the time I was seventeen, I was fed up with living at home. I decided to move, to find a flat of my own and have a bit of independence.

A semicolon is often described as a 'supercomma' – it separates two parts of a sentence that don't *quite* justify being sentences on their own:

She stood up and went to the window. The view was extraordinary; it never failed to lift her spirits.

You could, in that example, have written:

She stood up and went to the window. The view was extraordinary. It never failed to lift her spirits.

But that is a bit jerky: it isn't wrong, but those three short sentences produce a rather staccato effect. Alternatively, you could have gone for:

She stood up and went to the window. The view was extraordinary and it never failed to lift her spirits.

That isn't wrong either, but you might feel that two 'ands' in quick succession sound clumsy.

Note that a comma (*The view was extraordinary, it never failed to lift her spirits*) *would* have been wrong. The fact that you have two statements that could stand alone as sentences and don't form part of a longer list means that you have to separate them by something more powerful than a comma.

And what about a colon? Well, if you glance back over the previous couple of pages, you'll see that I have used them before my examples. That is their most common function – to introduce a list or to precede a piece of supplementary information:

There were four people in the car: Pat, Richard, Susie and a blonde woman I didn't recognize.

The shop had everything I had been looking for: art paper, gold paint and lots of paint brushes.

If the first part of your sentence makes your reader want to say, 'Tell me more. Explain yourself', chances are a colon is appropriate. But see also the section about dashes on page 61.

After a full stop, use a capital letter. After a semicolon or colon, use a lower-case letter unless the word would begin with a capital anyway.

Question marks and exclamation marks

Both of these should, in theory, be easy to deal with: they come at the end of a direct question or exclamation:

Where are we going?
What time is it?
How awful!
I'm so happy for you!

Confusion tends to arise when dealing with *indirect* versions of these questions and exclamations:

He asked where we were going.
I wonder what time it is.
She thought it was awful.
He said he was really happy for me.

These are statements, not questions or exclamations, and don't require the same punctuation – see the box.

The overuse of question and exclamation marks is dodgy ground. In early 2016, the UK Department for Education issued a ruling that students at Key Stage 2 level (about seven to eleven years old) should use exclamation marks only at the end of sentences beginning with 'What' or 'How', as in 'What a lovely day!' or 'How exciting!' With the greatest possible respect to the DfE, this advice, however well intentioned, is nonsense. It means you shouldn't use

FAQ – What's indirect speech?

Also known as reported speech, it's when you *report* what someone has said without quoting their words *directly*.

'I'm bored and I want to go home,' she said is direct speech. Reporting this indirectly would produce

She said she was bored and wanted to go home.

This statement doesn't require quotation marks.

Similarly, reporting a question or an exclamation doesn't require a question mark or an exclamation mark:

'Do you come from Melbourne?' she asked becomes *She asked if I came from Melbourne.*

'Look out!' he called becomes *He called to me to look out.*

In these reported examples, the main verbs are *she asked* and *he called* – statements rather than questions or exclamations, hence the change in punctuation. And because the verbs are in the past tense, what follows them goes into the past, too. You wouldn't say *She said she is bored and wants to go home*, although you would keep the present tense if the main verb was in the present: *She says she is bored and wants to go home.*

an exclamation mark for 'Look out! There's a car coming!' or 'Don't touch that! It's hot!' Yes, you could write those sentences with an emotionless full stop at the end, but that wouldn't convey the panic of a parent telling a child not to cross the street or to keep its hand away from the stove.

The real point is that – in formal writing – question marks and especially exclamation marks should be used sparingly. A single question mark at the end of a question shows that it is indeed a question, and what more could one want? As for exclamation marks, F. Scott Fitzgerald went further and observed that using them was like laughing at your own jokes. (He didn't say it was 'bad form', but that is obviously what he meant.)

As so often, informal communication has its own rules. It's perfectly okay to text someone '???' to mean 'I apologize for my apparent stupidity, but I have no idea what you are talking about' or '!!!' to suggest 'I am very excited to hear your news.' You can use multiple exclamations marks for comic effect, Batman-like (*Pow!! Kaboom!!!!*). You can even use a question mark followed by an exclamation mark (?!) to convey excited bafflement or wonder (*Do you really mean they're engaged at last?!*). But these are all casual, writing-to-a-friend, social contexts; that sort of gushing (and yes, believe me, punctuation can gush) is out of place in a job application or company report.

A final point about exclamation marks: use them too often and you lose the impact. Not everything you write is worth exclaiming about. A five-star review of one of my books on Amazon reads: *'I keep on dipping in and out of it!!! I can't put it down!! A perfect present for students and a great book to put in the Christmas stocking!'* I'm delighted, of course. Who wouldn't be pleased to have one of their books greeted with such enthusiasm? But – and I'm happy to range myself on the side of Scott Fitzgerald here – six exclamation marks in the space of three sentences is at least five too many.

Apostrophes

The twentieth century saw the rise of the much reviled 'greengrocer's apostrophe', with apostrophes turning up in words such as *tomatoe's* and *banana's*, where they had no business to be. The twenty-first century has gone one further and, in certain circles, called for the apostrophe to be abolished altogether – on the surely-not-very-flattering-to-most-of-us grounds that it is 'too difficult' for people to understand.

Oh, *puh-leeze*.

Shortly after I'd written that, I came across an advertisement for a ferry company inviting me to *reserve this years'* [sic] *sailings* by paying a small deposit. A day or two later a colleague emailed to ask if I could help her with something and ended her message *Finger's crossed* (an anatomical impossibility, I'd have thought). So clearly there is confusion out there. If you happen to be one of the confused, skip forward to page 55, but don't forget to come back.

Whole books have been written about the use and misuse of apostrophes, which seems to me to add fuel to the 'it's all too difficult' fire. But it isn't. It really isn't.

The rules can be summarized, in perhaps a rather simplistic way, as 'The apostrophe does two things. It indicates possession or association; and it indicates that a letter is missing.' Yes, of course, there is more to it than that, and you can dig back into Old English if you like, but it'll do as a rule of thumb so is fine as a starting point.

Possession and association

If you want to show that something belongs to or is in some way connected with a (single) person or thing, add apostrophe + s to the 'owner':

> *David's football jersey* (= the football jersey belonging to David)
> *Beethoven's Fifth* (= the fifth symphony that Beethoven wrote)

the doctor's surgery (= the surgery where a lone doctor works)

If it belongs to more than one person or thing, indicated by a plural ending in s, add an apostrophe *after* the s:

the boys' football kit (= the kit belonging to the boys; if it was an individual boy it would be *boy's*)
the composers' works (= the works of Beethoven, Bach and all the rest of them; if you are just talking about Beethoven it is *the composer's works*)
the doctors' surgery (there is more than one doctor)

When a plural doesn't end in s, add apostrophe + s:

children's games (= the games that children play)
the geese's honking (= the honking sound that the geese make)

This applies even when the plural is the same as the singular: *sheep's clothing* could refer to any number of sheep, or to just the one – you have to work this out from the context. The point to remember is that the plural of *sheep* is *sheep*, not *sheeps*, so you can't have *sheeps' clothing*, however many wolves you are trying to fit into it.

If the singular form of a noun ends in *h*, *s*, *x* or *z*, the plural normally requires an *–es* ending rather than just *–s* (*one church, two churches*; *one address, a book* *of addresses*; *one fox, a troop of foxes*; *one waltz, a dance programme full of waltzes*). None of these requires an apostrophe *unless you want to indicate possession or association*: *the fox's barking* (just the one fox), *the foxes' barking* (likely to be pretty noisy). The sign on a hoarding round my local shopping centre advising me that *business's are open as usual* had slipped in a random and unnecessary piece of punctuation.

If you're in doubt about any of this, rephrase in your mind to include an *of*: the barking of the fox? Add *'s*. The barking of the foxes? Add *s'*.

Complications arise with *names* ending in *s*, though: do you add apostrophe + s or just the apostrophe? *Dickens' novels* or *Dickens's novels*? *James' style* or *James's style*? There is no hard and fast rule about this, but generally speaking use apostrophe + s with words of up to two syllables (*Tess's bank account, Thomas's debts*) and just the apostrophe with longer ones (*Coriolanus' mother, Demetrius' lover*).

If a name ends in *–ses*, whether singular or plural, or if the last syllable is pronounced *–eeze*, stick to the apostrophe: *Moses' commandments, the Joneses' party, Socrates' questions*.

And, if it all starts to become a bit of a mouthful, rephrase: *the plays of Aristophanes*; *the death of Marcus Brutus.*

> ## We'll still have each other
>
> Apply the same logic as for *sheep* and you'll see that in an expression such as *the boys used to spend a lot of time in each other's houses*, the apostrophe goes before the *s*. However many houses there may be, they are the *houses of each other*, not *of each others*. Hence the *'s*.

It's my name and I'll do what I like

Place names are a law unto themselves: in London, Earl's Court has an apostrophe but Barons Court does not; St James's Park is also in London, while Newcastle United play football at St James' Park and Exeter City's home ground is St James Park. King's Cross in London has an apostrophe; Kings Cross in Sydney does not. If there is a logic to that, I'd love to know what it is.

Also a law unto himself, of course, was the Irish writer James Joyce. His novel *Finnegans Wake* has no apostrophe in its title, allowing scholars and those who should get out more to wonder whether it refers to carousing after the funeral of an individual named Finnegan, or is an exhortation to a group of people called Finnegan to awake and perhaps shake off the shackles of their history. We have a choice, in other words, between *Finnegan's Wake* and *Finnegans, Wake!* Joyce said of this extraordinary book, 'I've put in so many enigmas and puzzles that it will keep the professors arguing for centuries over what I meant. And that's the only way of assuring one's immortality.' He's probably rocking with laughter in his Swiss grave at the very thought of my typing this paragraph.

FAQ – What's the difference between its and it's?

There is a class of words called possessive determiners which – like so many other things in this book – really aren't as scary as they sound. They are words such as *my*, *your*, *his*, *her*, *its*, *our* and *their* and they are used in sentences such as:

My story is a sad one.
This is your song.
His name is Pierre.
I have to brush our dog every day

and, most significantly:

Its coat gets very tatty if I don't.

Probably the single most overlooked or misunderstood rule about apostrophes is that *it's* is short for *it is* or *it has*. I'm going to put this in bold: **there is no apostrophe in the possessive form *its***. Look at the different meanings of *it's* and *its* in these examples:

> *It's a long story, but wait till you hear its punch line.*
> *It's a beautiful dress: I particularly like its lacy sleeves.*
> *The lion has amazing vocal cords: its roar carries eight kilometres. It's got the loudest roar of any cat.*

There are also a number of personal pronouns that end in *s* and don't have apostrophes:

> *My coat is grey; hers is the blue one.*
> *Our holiday doesn't sound nearly as exciting as theirs.*
> *I've finished my book; may I borrow yours?*

But to repeat one hard and fast rule: *it's* has an apostrophe only when it is short for *it is* or *it has*.

Something missing

You'll notice that, so far, all the words I've been attaching apostrophes to are nouns. But when it comes to their second function – indicating that something has been left out – they occur mostly commonly in verbal contractions.

Doh?

Sorry. I mean words such as *won't, can't, shan't, isn't, aren't*. If you write these words out formally they all end in *not*: *will not, cannot, shall not, is not, are not*. In speech and in casual writing we abbreviate them, and the apostrophes indicate that the *o* of *not* is missing.

Then there is: *It's a bit of a challenge, she's standing in the way, he's either going to run over that pheasant or drive into the ditch.* The apostrophes here indicate the missing *i* in *it is, she is, he is.*

We're going to be late; I'll phone to see if they've left yet. The apostrophes show that there are letters missing from *we are, I will* (or *shall*), *they have.*

And take note of the difference between *your* and *you're. Your* is the possessive determiner mentioned on page 51; *you're* is short for *you are*:

One argument in favour of apostrophes

If we were to abandon them, think what confusion there would be in the use of words such as *wont, cant, well, ill, hell, shell* and *were.* Okay, it is not difficult to tell from the context the difference between, say, *We found a pretty shell on the beach* and *If you ask her nicely, shell drive you to the station*, or *Hell for leather* and *Hell be with you in a minute.* But, as with my 'I was in a state of course' example earlier, it might make a reader pause for a moment to work out what you mean. That would interrupt the flow of his or her reading and, as an author, you dont (or donut) want that, do you?

Do go and put your coat on. You're going to be late.
You're looking gorgeous: that blue dress makes your
eyes sparkle.
You should keep a better hold on your temper: you're
always shouting at people.

Apostrophes also show that something has been left out of dates: *the 1980s and '90s*. But they aren't necessary when an *s* is added to a date or to an abbreviation to make a plural: *the 1950s*, *my collection of CDs*, *PDFs*. Nor, to revert to the subject of greengrocers, are they required in plurals simply because a word ends in a vowel: there may well be confusion about whether or not to put an *e* in *avocados*, *bananas*, *potatoes* or *tomatoes*, but there is definitely no need for an apostrophe.

If in doubt, remind yourself of the rules given above and ask yourself if inserting an apostrophe would serve a purpose. If not, leave it out.

One druid or two?

One of the many facets of the anti-apostrophe argument is, apparently, that they confuse the emergency services, who run the risk of turning up in Druid's Cross when the fire is in Druids' Cross. While I hope that not even the most hardened pedant would risk endangering people's lives for the sake of getting apostrophes right, it can surely not be beyond the wit of modern technology to devise a system that omits and ignores apostrophes in Satnavs while allowing them to remain on road signs and those wrought-iron plaques that welcome us to historic villages. After all, how likely is it that the same fire service will have within its jurisdiction a street called, say, Druid's Avenue (where only one druid used to hang out) and another called Druids' Avenue (where a number of druids got together)? And if it does:

1) Surely the emergency vehicle is going to be confused anyway, wherever anyone puts the apostrophes and

2) Isn't that why postcodes were invented?

Apostrophes are only difficult if we allow ourselves to believe that they are.

If you are still wondering what was wrong with the two examples I gave at the beginning of this section on apostrophes, *this year's sailings* (apostrophe before the s) would have been correct: it means *the sailings that are taking place this* [singular] *year. Fingers crossed* is simply shorthand for *my fingers are crossed* and needs no apostrophe at all.

Hyphens

In the 1880s, the Metropolitan Police produced a poster bearing what it called a *fac-simile* of a letter that was a key piece of evidence in an investigation; it asked anyone who recognized the handwriting to get in touch. In the seventeenth century, when this term (meaning an exact copy) came into English, it was written as two words, acknowledging its Latin origins: etymologically it was a command or imperative – 'Make something like this.' As the concept became more familiar it began to be written with a hyphen and eventually as one word. Did the average 1980s office worker, sending the ubiquitous *fax* of pre-email days, give a thought to the fact that this useful little word was a contraction of a Latin command?

Post mortem – the examination of a dead body, usually to determine the cause of death – has had an interesting life, not to say a rather convoluted one. It's Latin for *after death* and was originally an adverbial phrase: *the examination took place post mortem.* Then it became an adjectival phrase, mostly used in medical contexts: *post mortem stiffness, post mortem bruising*, but not hyphenated because the medical folk using it were writing it in Latin. Then it became more familiar, more widely used and was treated as English, where the two-word adjective requires a hyphen. So we find *the post-mortem examination* and, in due course, simply a *post-mortem* or *post mortem*. The use of two words, with or without the hyphen, continues to acknowledge the term's Latin roots, and both these forms are found in dictionaries. The *Guardian* crossword, however, in early 2016, had *postmortem* as a one-word solution. It provoked some discussion on a solvers' forum, but it can't be long before this too becomes the norm.

Hyphens are often a sign that a term is a recent coinage, with the hyphen disappearing as the new word gains acceptance (and its origins are, perhaps, forgotten). *Today*, *tonight* and *tomorrow* were once all two words, the *to* being an old use of the preposition that conveys the sense of 'at a time, on a day'. Both *to day* and *to night* have been around for a thousand years, *to morrow* nearly as long, but they weren't often written as one word until the twentieth century and I've seen *to-day* with a hyphen in a novel published in 1948 and *to-morrow* as late as 1959. Other such commonplace words as *newspaper* and *racehorse* have also sometimes had hyphens in the course of their history.

We've seen the same phenomenon more recently when first *e-mail* and then *e-books* appeared: they were initially written with inverted commas (*'e-mail'*, *'e-books'* or possibly *'e'-mail*, *'e'-books*) to indicate that the author acknowledged them as new coinages; as the terms became more familiar, the inverted commas disappeared, followed by the hyphens, until finally

You don't scare me

The inverted commas round new coinages such as 'e-mail' are what journalists call 'scare quotes'. They show that the author is distancing herself from what is being quoted. Arty terms such as 'impressionist' and 'cubist', originally used disparagingly, were at first written in this way: it was politer than saying 'the so-called impressionists', but only just.

Here, as in everything else about language, times and fashions change. In 1952, the BBC, rejecting an offer of services from Mrs Barbara Woodhouse, who later became a household name for her idiosyncratic approach to dog training, referred to 'a great number of similar applications from "would-be" commentators'. To a modern eye, that looks very odd. Fifty years later, equally pompous writers who didn't happen to be fans of the Spice Girls could have written 'applications from "wannabe" commentators' in the same dismissive way. Yet *wannabe* has become so commonplace that we can use it – of, for example, competitors on a television talent show – without even specifying what it is that these seekers after fame and fortune *want to be*.

the words were accepted in their own right. We now ignore the fact that the *e* stands for *electronic* (just as we ignore the Latin origins of *facsimile*) and write them as *email* and *ebooks*. As I type this, though, Microsoft Word introduces a squiggly red line of non-recognition under *ebooks* (for reasons of its own, it prefers eBooks), but is quite happy with *email*. By the time I upgrade, it will probably have learned to live with *ebooks* too.

Similarly, *sound bite* (a bite-sized turn of phrase used in a speech or interview by a politician in the hope of its being quoted) has been around only since the 1980s and in the course of its short life has sometimes merited a hyphen. But it is so widely used in our modern quick-fire world that it is now routinely seen written as one word and the spin-off *news bite* (a bite-sized chunk of news suitable for being read online) can't be far behind. I've also recently seen both *standalone* and *taskforce* as one word, though neither the OED nor Chambers yet acknowledges them. But they will, they will.

None of this may seem very important, because there is no question of ambiguity in any of it. It's a matter of an author's or publisher's preferred style. But with compound expressions, especially compound adjectives, there often is ambiguity, and the hyphen comes into its own: it shows that the hyphenated words are linked and should be interpreted as a single entity. For example:

● *Fast food retailers* probably sell burgers and the like,

but without hyphenating *fast-food* you can't be sure: they could be speedy retailers of any type of food.

- *Intelligent-design theorists* oppose Darwin's views on evolution; *intelligent design theorists* are clever people who have theories about design.

- A *hard-working wife* puts in long hours; a *hard working wife* goes to the office but isn't a very sympathetic person.

- *Four weekly reports* are very different from *four-weekly reports*: the first means four reports, delivered once a week; the second an unspecified number of reports, delivered at intervals of four weeks.

- And I recently noticed *short hand typing*, which sounds as if you can't do it if you happened to have long hands.

Finally, a word from an expert: in J. D. Salinger's story *Seymour: an Introduction*, the narrator is a college lecturer who at one point mentions *the sixty odd girls (or, that is, the sixty-odd girls)* in one of his classes. It's a pedant's joke: either might be accurate, but by inserting the hyphen the narrator tells us that he is making no comment on the personalities of his students, merely assessing how many of them there are.

A dash of glamour

A hyphen, by the way, is different from a dash. For a start it is shorter: - as opposed to – or —. And its use is completely different. A single dash indicates a break in a train of thought, or introduces an additional piece of information:

You'd better go home – you'll be late for dinner.
It's not the exams I worry about – it's what I do when they're over.
The article was full of silly mistakes – a sure sign that no one had bothered to check the facts.

Or it shows that there are words left unspoken:

I'm not saying he's a liar, but –

In this instance, an ellipsis – dot dot dot – would serve the same purpose: *I'm not saying he's a liar, but . . .*

A pair of dashes acts like the pairs of commas or pairs of brackets we saw earlier (see pages 34–6) – they enclose a piece of information that is not grammatically essential to the sentence, however fascinating it may be:

He looked at the guest list – the usual mix of hangers-on and has-beens – and realized he was in for another boring evening.

The room showed all the signs of good housekeeping – a beautifully polished table, an immaculately made bed – but it wasn't exactly cosy.

A single dash can often be replaced by a colon or semicolon; a pair by a pair of commas. It's a matter of taste, but dashes tend to give a more casual feel and should be used sparingly. Too many of them make your writing look – well, a bit slapdash.

CHAPTER 3

Grammar rules (OK?)

*Why some of them are made
to be broken*

Those who believe that the English language is going to the dogs routinely cite *Thou shalt not split an infinitive* and *Thou shalt not end a sentence with a preposition* as rules that are regularly broken even by people who know what infinitives and prepositions are. Those who oppose rigid adherence to old-fashioned rules cite the same commandments as two of the most absurd with which we have hidebound ourselves.

In first position

To deal with the prepositional question first, a poster in my local travel agent asks the question 'Where would you like to fly to?' and, on a gloomy February day, offers such appealing possibilities as St Lucia, Mauritius and Cape Town. I can be as pedantic as the next person, but I don't think 'To where would you like to fly?' or 'Whither would you like to fly?' would have pulled in many punters.

To expand on what I said on page 12, prepositions are generally those little words that relate a noun (or something that acts like a noun – see the examples below) to the rest of the sentence. They often refer to time or place, but may also explain reasons, give additions and exceptions, and express support or opposition:

- *I want to have a shower* before *the others arrive.*

- *They closed the stable door* after *the horse had bolted.*

- *He hid* behind *the desk* until *the banging stopped.*

- *She threw a stone* into *the water.*

- Despite *the sunshine, he was carrying an umbrella.*

- *The nurse comes every day* except *Tuesdays.*

- *He may talk too much, but don't hold that* against *him – he is very entertaining.*

I said 'generally' in the previous paragraph because there are also things called prepositional phrases. They behave like prepositions but consist of more than one word:

- *She let the old man go through the gate* ahead of *her.*

- With reference to *our conversation, I confirm that we agreed the following.*

- *Everyone voted* in favour of *adjourning the meeting.*

- *He spoke passionately* on behalf of *those who were unable to speak for themselves.*

The name *preposition* suggests that it should go *before* (*pre-*) something. In Latin this is true: prepositions always precede the noun. In English in formal writing it's worth aiming to stick to this 'rule' (I'm putting it in inverted commas because life is too short to argue about whether or not it is actually a rule): Noël Coward's patriotic Second World War film would have sounded rather less stirring if it had been called *Which We Serve In*. On the other hand, in speech and in more casual writing, as in the travel agent example given a few paragraphs ago, refusing to end a sentence with a preposition often produces something absurd. If you want to avoid saying, 'There was no one at the conference worth listening to' you need to become quite convoluted: 'There was no one at the conference to whom it was worth listening.' If a friend complained to you that he had lost money in a dodgy poker game, you might reply, 'You ought to be more careful who you play with'; you'd be unlikely to suggest he be more careful with whom he plays. And if you were asking a client for a deadline, you wouldn't say – or write, however formal you were being – 'By when do you need it?'

One instance when it is awkward or even wrong to avoid ending a sentence with a preposition is when a clause contains two verbs, only one of which requires a preposition:

> *The syllabus included topics about which the students could study and talk* is clearly wrong – the *about* goes with *talk*, but not with *study.*

> *The syllabus included topics which the students could study and about which they could talk* is correct but very heavy.

> *... topics they could study and talk about* sounds much more natural.

The great H. W. Fowler (in his *Dictionary of Modern English Usage*, first published in 1926) sums it up perfectly when he says, '... in respect of elegance or inelegance, every example must be judged not by any arbitrary rule, but on its own merits, according to the impression it makes on the feeling of educated English readers.' There's a soupçon of snobbery there, perhaps, but only a soupçon.

I'll look into that

English has a number of multi-word verbs that include a preposition. Many of these are transitive verbs, meaning that they take a direct object (page 68), which comes after the preposition:

- The police promised to *look into* the complaint.

It makes all the difference

Fowler put people's mind at rest about another question that causes anxiety. He says – and who are we to disagree? – that *different to* and *different from* are both acceptable in British English.

On the other hand, most British pundits object to *different than*, which is much used in American English. If they have an explanation for this, it tends to be that *than* introduces a comparison (*he is older than me*, *the pen is mightier than the sword*) and describing something as *different* is not the same as making a comparison.

Argue that one if you like, but given that we have two acceptable options, do we need to fight about a third?

- His accent was so strong I couldn't *make out* what he was saying.

- If you can't come I'll find someone to *stand in for* you.

But sometimes the multi-word verb is intransitive – it doesn't have a direct object – and then the 'don't end a sentence with a preposition' brigade is in trouble:

I was fascinated by what she was saying and begged her to go on.

When a teacher comes into the room the students are supposed to stand up.
Please sit down *and* shut up.

There is no avoiding ending sentences such as these with a preposition. Don't even begin to worry about it.

I have no objection

To expand a little on the idea of transitive and intransitive verbs, a *transitive verb* needs a direct object for it to completely make sense (see pages 13–14 if you aren't sure what a direct object is). An *intransitive verb* is complete in itself:

I worried.
You were sleeping.
He will succeed.

These are all complete, sensible sentences. Yes, you can qualify these verbs (*I worried about the future, you were sleeping deeply, he will succeed to the throne*), but none of these additions is a direct object. Compare:

I kicked.
You built.
He touches.

With all of these you want to ask the question 'What?'

What did I kick? What did you build? What is he touching? *The ball, the house, his toes,* perhaps, or indeed *his shin, a castle in the air, the ceiling* – it doesn't matter. The point is that the verb needs the object in order to convey its full meaning.

Just to keep you on your toes, some verbs can be either transitive or intransitive:

The lie of the land

Massive confusion exists between the verbs *lay* and *lie*, but much of it can be eased once you remember that *lay* is transitive and *lie* is intransitive. In other words, you have to lay *something* – an egg, the table, a hand on someone's shoulder. You *lie on a bed* or simply *lie down*, or *you lie through your teeth* when you are telling an untruth.

In the past tense, you *laid the table* or *lied through your teeth*, but (in further confusion) *lay on your bed.* The past participles are *lain* for *he had lain the table* or *she had lain on her bed* but *lied* for *they had lied so often that we couldn't believe they were telling the truth this time.*

As for title of this box, *the lie of the land* is the way the land (intransitively) *lies. Lay* as a noun means a song or ballad.

I haven't read much poetry (transitive, *much poetry* being the object); *I was reading all afternoon* (intransitive – all afternoon isn't an object, it's an adverbial phrase answering the question 'when?').

I can dance the tango (transitive, *the tango* being the object); *I used to dance with my sister* (intransitive).

As for direct and indirect objects, I said on page 13 that a simple sentence has a subject, a verb and an object. The object is the person or thing on which the action of the verb is performed:

I paid the bill.
We are watching television.
They broke the rules.

The bill, *television* and *the rules* are all *direct objects*. A verb may also have an *indirect object* – something which is affected by the action of the verb, but not directly. Indirect objects are often introduced by *to* or *for*:

I gave a letter *to the postman.*
He brought a gift *for his host.*
They showed the prescription *to the pharmacist.*

Letter, *gift* and *prescription* are the direct objects, the italicized words are the indirect objects. These sentences can all be rephrased to dispense with the preposition, again with the indirect objects shown in italics:

I gave *the postman* a letter.
He brought *his host* a gift.
They showed *the pharmacist* the prescription.

The same applies if the indirect object is a pronoun:

I'll pay the difference *to her*/I'll pay *her* the difference.
Please save a seat *for me*/please save *me* a seat.

A direct object answers the question 'What?':

What did I give to the postman? A letter.
What did he bring for his host? A gift.

An indirect object answers questions such as 'To whom?' 'For whom?':

To whom will I pay the difference? To her.
For whom should I save a seat? For you.

To split or not to split

On the subject of splitting infinitives, Fowler wrote that *the English-speaking world may be divided into (1) those who neither know nor care what a split infinitive is; (2) those who do not know but care very much; (3) those who know & condemn; (4) those who know & approve; (5) those who know & distinguish.*

Those who neither know nor care, he continues, *are the vast majority, & are a happy folk ... 'to really*

FAQ – What is an adverb?

Adverbs and adverbial phrases and clauses answer questions such as *how?*, *why?*, *when?* and *where?* and describe the way the action of the verb is performed:

He spoke sadly (*sadly* qualifies the verb *spoke* and explains *how* he spoke).

I was late because the car broke down (*because the car broke down* explains *why* you were late).

We are coming the day after tomorrow (answering the question '*When* are you coming?').

They went skiing in the Alps (telling us *where* they went skiing).

Adverbs also describe or qualify adjectives and other adverbs:

The scenery was stunningly *beautiful* (qualifying the adjective *beautiful*).

He moved very cautiously (*cautiously* describing the verb and answering the question 'How did he move?'; *very* qualifying the adverb *cautiously*).

And why do we care? Because when you split an infinitive the word that does the splitting is likely to be an adverb. Read on.

understand' comes readier to their lips & pens than 'really to understand', they see no reason why they should not say it . . . & they do say it.

Happy folk indeed, for they don't lose sleep over whether or not it is acceptable to say *to clearly establish*, *to really believe* or *to absolutely forbid.*

For the benefit of those who don't know but may care, I should explain that the infinitive is what is called the base form of the verb, usually preceded by *to*. An infinitive conveys meaning – we know what *to play* or *to laugh* means – but it doesn't specify number or tense. It can be inflected (given different endings) to produce *finite verbs*, which do convey number and tense: *he plays* (singular present), *they laughed* (plural past, although we know it is plural only because of the *they*; the singular *I laughed* and *he laughed* use the same verb form). Or it may be preceded by one or more auxiliary (helping) verbs to produce other tenses – *I will be*, *you may proceed* – or a combination of the two – *he has forgotten*, *we should have replied.* But it is the basic form, preceded by *to*, that we mean when we discuss splitting infinitives.

One argument against splitting an infinitive is that many people believe you shouldn't, so they will criticize your use of English if you do. The other is that the outcome is ugly or inelegant or some other subjective word. I recently read something in a newspaper about *expecting business models to further adapt and change*, a split which struck me as both unnecessary and probably inaccurate. The positioning of *further* suggests that it applies only to *adapt*, whereas it's a reasonable assumption that both the adapting and the changing are ongoing. *To adapt and change further*, with *further* applying to both verbs, would have been fine. *Further to adapt and change* would have been accurate but rather formal. Perhaps the best option, as is often the case with tricky grammatical points, would have been to avoid the problem by going for *to continue to adapt and change*.

Arguments for the other camp invoke the twin horrors of ambiguity and clumsiness. The ambiguity of *A security guard who installed a camera secretly to film anyone entering the lab* ... is caused by the desperate fear of splitting an infinitive. What was it that was done secretly? The installation or the filming? (Or, given the context, perhaps both?) *Who secretly installed* or *to secretly film* would have sorted this out, while ... *to film anyone secretly entering the lab* would have given the sentence a new and sinister twist.

In terms of clumsiness or daintiness, there's not much to choose between *to strengthen the economy further* and *to further strengthen the economy*, but what if your sentence is more complex than that? If you throw up your hands in horror at *to further strengthen the economies of the world's emergent nations*, where should you put the adverb?

A joy of adverbs is that their positioning is often quite flexible:

> *further to strengthen the economies of the world's emergent nations*
>
> *to strengthen further the economies of the world's emergent nations*
>
> *to strengthen the economies of the world's emergent nations further*

All are 'correct' and all mean the same thing. You may feel that one sounds better than another, that for some reason it has a more pleasing flow or rhythm, but that is a matter of taste and style rather than accuracy.

When I say 'often quite flexible', though, I do mean often. Not always. Consider *Running uphill quickly builds up muscle tone.* What is it that is happening quickly? The running? Or the building up of muscle tone? There's nothing to tell us. *Quickly running uphill* or *builds up muscle tone quickly* would have been unambiguous. If there is any risk of doubt, put the adverb as close as possible to the word it qualifies.

Adverbial phrases can pose a similar problem. Groucho Marx famously quipped, 'I once shot an elephant in my pyjamas. How he got into my pyjamas I'll never know.' But he was clearly well aware of what he was saying. When takeaway food was a novelty, however, it was sometimes explained that 'we serve our curries to customers in boxes', prompting the witty to retort that they weren't planning to turn up in a box, and even if they were they would prefer not to share it with a curry. Unambiguous versions of these remarks may turn out to be a bit more long-winded: 'I once shot an elephant while I was still in my pyjamas'; 'We serve our curries in boxes for customers to take away'; but if they avoid others making wisecracks at your expense, it's a small price to pay.

Here are two other examples where paying more attention to word order would have helped:

> *The last major retrospective of his work was held six years after his death in 1988 at the Serpentine Gallery.*

Contrary to what you might assume from this, the artist concerned died in 1982, and he didn't pass away at the Serpentine Gallery. Commas after *death* and *1988* would have made that a bit clearer, but rephrasing to *The last major retrospective of his work was held at the Serpentine Gallery in 1988, six years after his death* would have been even better.

A historian writing about *the threat to the security and stability of British life from abroad* left her readers wondering what 'British life from abroad' was. Again, *the threat from abroad to the security and stability of British life* leaves the quibblers with nothing to quibble about (or about which to quibble).

Little words mean a lot

At one point in his wonderful book *Mail Obsession*, my friend Mark Mason is about to travel by ferry from Aberdeen to Shetland. Checking the shipping forecast, he finds that *Cromarty and Fair Isle, through which I'll be travelling tonight, look as though they'll hold few terrors*.

He's relieved – who wouldn't be? But what if he'd added a simple *a* before the word *few*? He wouldn't have been so cheerful, would he?

Extrapolating from that, I wonder if there was *little chance of a storm* that night (meaning it wasn't likely to happen) or *a little chance* (in which case it might well).

Consider also *your performance was little short of magnificent*. You'd almost certainly be delighted if someone said that to you. If they said your performance was *a little short of magnificent*, you'd be mortified, both by their opinion and by their sarcastic way of expressing it. No wonder English is so difficult for non-native speakers to learn.

Little spaces can mean a lot, too. There's a world of difference between:

I don't want to be involved in any way (I am firmly keeping my distance)

and

I don't want to be involved anyway (you can say what you like but you won't persuade me).

There's also a difference between the adverb *maybe* (meaning *perhaps*) and the verb *may be* (meaning variations on the theme of *it is possible that*):

Maybe I'm being over-cautious . . .
There may be troubles ahead . . .

Few people now bother about the distinction between *for ever* and *forever*, though some would say that *forever* was an Americanism, in British English to be used only as a rather poetic noun (*the great unknown forever*, meaning death) or a more casual one (*it took me forever to get here*).

Nonetheless and *nevertheless* are both single words when they mean 'all the same, despite what has just been said'. *None the less* becomes three words when it means 'no less' in sentences such as *He means well but is none the less irritating for that*.

And, while it is really cheating to include 'misprints spotted around the world' in a book such as this, I couldn't resist the announcement that 'lunch will be gin at 12.30 p.m.' It seems to belong in a sort Ernest Hemingway world in which breakfast might well be whisky at 9 a.m.

Could I get a . . .

. . . single-shot skinny latte, for example? When did we start saying this? And why? Even if you ignore the old-fashioned, U-and-non-U attitude that 'get' isn't a word (which is nonsense, of course, but it isn't an elegant word and if you're writing or saying anything formal it's worth trying to find an alternative) and replace it with the more-acceptable-to-the-older-generation 'have', you're losing a useful distinction between *can* and *may/could* and *might*.

Can and *could* tell us whether or not a thing is possible; *may* and *might* deal with permission. If you ask a purist, '*Can* I borrow your pearl necklace for the party?', she may reply, 'If you can take it from my jewel case without my catching you.' If you ask, '*May* I borrow', she will have no opportunity to be sarcastic and with any luck will lend it to you without further ado.

Confusingly, *may* and *might* indicate possibility when the subject under discussion is undecided:

I may *lend her my necklace: I haven't made up my mind.*

I might *lend her my necklace if she lets me borrow her red handbag.*

In this second example, you may still refuse to lend the necklace, whatever happens about the handbag. You're still pondering. If you've decided in favour, it becomes:

> *I* shall *lend her my necklace if she lets me borrow her red handbag.*

This raises another pernickety point. Lots of people would say *I* will *lend*, but the purists' rule is *I* or *we shall, you/he/she/it/they will.* For emphasis, it becomes the other way round:

> *I* will *go out this evening* (even though I am still recovering from a cold).
> *You* shall *go to the ball* (against all the odds).

This applies in the negative too:

> *I* shan't *be able to come, I'm afraid* (no particular emphasis).
> *I* won't *go, however often you ask* (so you might as well stop bothering me).

Voices

Here's another instance of definitions being scarier than they need to be. You wouldn't have thought *voices* were scary at all unless you'd just been watching Jack Nicholson in *The Shining*. But read the definition: 'a category used in the classification of verb forms serving to indicate the relation of the subject to the action'. Eek.

What it boils down to is this: a verb can be either *active voice* or *passive voice*, and those two terms mean pretty much what you might expect them to mean. An active verb does something; a passive verb suffers/ endures/is the recipient of the action:

A newcomer won the marathon is active: the newcomer did the winning.

The marathon was won by a newcomer is passive: the marathon had the winning done to it.

Generally speaking, as you might expect, active verbs make for punchier, more active sentences, but the passive comes into its own when you don't know who is performing the action:

The speaker was bombarded with tomatoes (you don't know who was doing the bombarding, and it sounds a bit silly to say *tomatoes bombarded the speaker*).

When I came into the kitchen I found that the washing-up had already been done (some kind but unknown kitchen fairy has appeared in the night).

Moods

Then there are moods. In the 1958 film *Gideon of Scotland Yard*, Inspector Gideon, facing a man with a gun in his hand, warns him, 'There's a police car outside with two men in it. And if you were fool enough to fire that gun ...' The other replies, 'I don't see why you should speak in the subjunctive. I *am* going to fire this gun.'

It's hard to imagine a scriptwriter coming up with a line like that nowadays, but it's an excellent example of what we mean by the *subjunctive mood*. In grammar a mood is defined as 'the form of a verb indicating whether it expresses fact, command or wish, etc.' and in English there are three of them.

When the mood takes you

Some describe the infinitive as a mood, too, but the OED qualifies this by adding 'though strictly a substantive with certain verbal functions, esp. those of governing an object, and being qualified by an adverb'. Did I mention that the explanations were scarier than they needed to be?

The indicative mood covers most ordinary statements and questions, whether past, present or future, positive or negative:

I don't want to go to work today.
You will be the only person missing.
She was in a foul temper.
Who cares?

The imperative mood deals with orders and instructions, even if they are politely expressed:

Stop being so silly.
Go and get dressed.
Please pass the butter.

But it's the subjunctive that causes most anxiety, because some of its forms look illogical or 'wrong'. Verbs in the subjunctive express doubt, fear or possibility, and occur in expressions such as *If I were you*. You'd think it should be *was*, to agree with the singular *I*, but that *were* is not a plural, it's a subjunctive singular. You use *were* after *I* or *he*, *she* or *it* if you are considering a possibility or talking about something you know to be untrue or in an uncertain future:

If I were you [which we know isn't true]*, I would jump at the chance.*
I wish I were in your shoes [but I'm not].
If it were possible [you never know – that rich uncle might leave you a fortune], *I'd sign up to fly to the moon.*
If he were to arrive on time [which he might, but we can't be sure], *we could go for a walk before dinner.*

Note that this last example has a different tone from the indicative *If he arrives on time, we can go for a walk before dinner.* The indicative is cheerful, optimistic; the subjective suggests we shouldn't hold our breath or put our boots on just yet.

Oh, and I don't suppose I am giving too much away if I tell you that the police burst in and the man with the gun *doesn't* shoot Inspector Gideon.

Spoiler alert

They didn't use this expression when *Gideon of Scotland Yard* was made, although *spoiler* in the sense of giving away the ending dates back to 1971, when *National Lampoon* published a selection of them 'guaranteed to reduce the risk of unsettling and possibly dangerous suspense . . .' If you haven't seen *Psycho*, look away now, because one of their spoilers was 'The movie's multiple murders are committed by Anthony Perkins disguised as his long-dead mother.' If you were (subjunctively) now to see the film for the first time, you wouldn't have to sit so close to the edge of your seat.

FAQ – Why do people make a fuss about only?

Despite what I said earlier about positioning adverbs wherever you like, the example about running uphill makes an important point: that moving the adverb around can change meaning. Many people routinely say things like *Oscar only works five minutes away* when what they mean is *Oscar works only five minutes away*. The first sentence, strictly speaking, is saying that *all* Oscar does five minutes away is work – he doesn't play, socialize, eat or drink. What is meant, of course, is that his office is a short distance away: *only* applies to *five minutes*, not to *works*. (The point becomes clearer, perhaps, if you move the adverb again. *Only Oscar works five minutes away* indicates that everyone else has to travel farther.)

At first glance, this may not seem to matter much, and often it doesn't. If someone says, *You can only come to the party if you dress properly* rather than the more correct *You can come to the party only if you dress properly*, you're unlikely to misunderstand them. But what about *She'll only improve her French if she spends time in France*? That *probably* means *She'll improve her French only if she spends time in France* – in other words, spending time in France is the only way for her to improve her French. But strictly speaking what it *says* is that all that will happen if she goes to France is that she will improve her French. She won't, the speaker implies, improve her maths or her IT skills. Or, if you say the sentence aloud in a disparaging tone, it could mean that if she goes to France, her French will improve – which is the last thing anyone wants.

A lot of this can be dismissed as nit-picking, but it is worth knowing the rules, because every now and again they *do* make a difference.

By way of comparison

A comparative compares two things; a superlative three or more. A short adjective is made into a comparative by adding *–er* and a superlative by adding *–est* (changing *y* to *i* if the original word ends in *y*). Thus:

That rock is big.
My rock is bigger *than your rock.*
The Rock of Gibraltar is the biggest *of all.*

That is a lovely *song.*
I think this one is even lovelier.
It is the loveliest *song ever written.*

With adjectives of more than two syllables, and with most adverbs, express the comparison by using *more* (or *less*) and *most* (or *least*):

Your garden is more beautiful *than mine.*
In fact, it is the most beautiful *in town.*

I'm trying to go out less often.
All the recipes look delicious, but this one seems the least complicated.

The most common irregular comparatives and super-latives occur with the adjectives *good* and *bad*. If something is *good* it may get *better* and end up being the *best*; something that goes from *bad* to *worse* will eventually reach rock bottom and be the *worst* it can be.

The points to remember here are:

- the comparative makes a comparison between two (and only two) things: an *elder son* has only one younger brother, though he may be the *eldest* in a family that includes daughters.

- you need only one comparative or superlative to make your point: to say something like *there are relatively fewer women in full-time employment* is to duplicate effort. Either *relatively few women* or *fewer women* is ample.

This last is one of the rules that some people will tell you were made to be broken, or aren't rules at all. They may even cite the example of Shakespeare (in *Julius Caesar*) writing that the wound Brutus had inflicted on Caesar was 'the most unkindest cut of all'. But although we've been taught to believe that Shakespeare could do no wrong, he wasn't a grammarian: he was interested in speech, and how it sounds. (I'm quoting the great director of Shakespeare, Sir Peter Hall, here, lest you think I am committing blasphemy by criticizing the Bard.) He used words for his own dramatic and poetic purposes, not according to any sixteenth-century book of rules. So if you happen to be writing a compelling piece of oratory and want to 'break the rules' for

That's all well and good

Good is irregular not only in the way it forms its comparative and superlative (*better* and *best*, see pages 86–7), but in the way it forms its adverb. *Goodly*, although it looks as if it should mean 'in a good way', in fact means 'considerable, sizeable' as in *a goodly sum of money*. The adverb meaning 'in a good way' is *well*: *she played the piano well, I knew him well, let me know well in advance.*

But *well* is also used as an adjective meaning healthy, as in 'I'm very well, thank you.' Answering the question 'How are you?' with 'I'm good, thank you' raises hackles on the back of many necks. 'I'm good,' say those prickly people, 'means "I am well behaved" and it is surely not for the speaker to judge.'

They're right, of course, those prickly people: 'I'm good' should be avoided in formal circumstances. There's no denying, though, that it has become a useful expression: 'I'm good' has also become shorthand for 'No, I won't have another drink just now, thank you', 'I'm quite comfortable, neither too hot nor too cold' and various other social niceties of this kind.

dramatic impact, please feel free. Similarly, if you want to say *worser and worser* (or even *worserer and worserer*) for comic effect, go right ahead. But be aware that that is what you are doing – and be prepared for those who like rules to pick you up on it.

Oh, I do agree

There are many other points of grammar and usage that get pedants' backs up (get up pedants' backs?). Here's one of them.

A newspaper quotes a resident of Soho as saying, 'When I moved here I couldn't sleep because you'll have people always walking about, you'll have the glass collectors coming at four in the morning . . .'

If you heard someone say this in conversation you probably wouldn't give it a second thought. But if the speaker had had time to go back and edit his words, he might have preferred, 'I couldn't sleep because there were always people walking about; the glass collectors came at four in the morning . . .' Or he could have stuck to the first person: 'I couldn't sleep because I could always hear people walking about . . .' Or made the whole statement general: 'Until you get used to the noise, you can't sleep, because you'll have people always walking about, you'll have the glass collectors coming . . .'

That change from 'I' to 'you' in the original quote is awkward, but you know exactly what the speaker means and he wasn't pretending to be Proust.

Much worse, I think, is this sentence from an advertisement for knitwear sold online: not only has it made it into print, it forms part of the terms and conditions, so you might expect a degree of accuracy: *You can return any item within three months of purchasing providing it has not been worn or washed, still have their tags attached and in their original packaging.* The 'it' refers, of course, to 'any item' (singular), and there would have been no awkwardness at all about saying that *it* should still have *its* tags attached and be in *its* original packaging. This is, frankly, just careless and the person who wrote it should have their (or his or her) wrists firmly slapped.

Which leads neatly on to the issue of using *they* (or *them/their/themself/themselves*) as a singular.

It used to be that *they* was plural and *he/she/it* was singular. If the gender of the subject wasn't clear, *he* served for both: the masculine, it used to be said, embraced the feminine. Before about the 1960s, few people would have objected to sentences such as:

A doctor has to work long hours for several years before he attains the status of consultant.

In a noisy room, you may have to ask your companion to repeat what he has just said.

Although in terms of language usage it was understood that the *he* could apply equally to male and female doctors and to male and female companions, there was an underlying assumption that the doctor, if not the companion, was likely to be male. As a backlash against this inherent sexism came an insistence on *he or she* or *s/he*, which is all very well if it occurs only once in a sentence or paragraph, but can get a bit heavy if you stick to it rigidly:

> *In a noisy room, you may have to ask your companion to repeat what he or she has just said. If he or she has a soft voice, his or her remarks may be drowned out by other conversations and he or she may be unwilling to shout to make him or herself heard.*

This is where the 'singular' *they* comes in, and there's a lot to be said for it:

> *In a noisy room, you may have to ask your companion to repeat what they have just said. If they have a soft voice, their remarks may be drowned out by other conversations and they may be unwilling to shout to make themselves heard.*

It wouldn't work in anything as formal as a legal document, but for day-to-day use it is surely neater. In some contexts – in a textbook referring to students, perhaps – authors choose to use *he* in one chapter and *she* in the next, alternating throughout the book.

I realize that this can be only a personal opinion, but I find that a bit self-consciously politically correct. If you read this book carefully, you'll notice I have taken a random approach, while trying not to assume that all doctors are male and all librarians female.

I still agree – but notionally

That advertisement I quoted earlier, about *an* item being returned with *their* tag, was just plain wrong. But an article about the surprising success of an unglamorous English football team raised a more debatable point. It remarked, about two-thirds of the way through the season, that *Leicester were meant to have crashed out of the top four by now*.

Leicester *were*? Well, yes. And no.

In theory, the name of any team – even the plural-sounding Rangers, Yankees and Giants with which sports abound – is singular. As is the rugby team Leicester Tigers. The soccer club the article is talking about is Leicester City – absolutely and utterly singular, you'd have thought.

But English has a concept called *notional agreement* (as opposed to *formal agreement*), whereby a singular collective noun such as *team* is treated as plural when the members are deemed to be acting individually rather than as a whole:

The group is *due to arrive any minute* (everyone is on the same coach).

The group are *arriving between five and six* (they're travelling separately but will be here for happy hour).

The committee has *made its decision* (and no one disagreed, at least not in public).

The committee have *failed to reach agreement and two of the members have resigned* (the members are – perhaps unfortunately – acting as individuals).

I read recently in a crime novel, in which a key witness had gone missing:

No one seems to know where he is. His office haven't got a clue . . . the hotel are saying he checked out early this morning.

This seems to me absolutely fine: clearly it means 'the people in his office' and 'the staff at the hotel'. To say *his office* hasn't *got a clue* or *the hotel* is *saying* would be to treat the office and the hotel as physical structures, rather than groups of employees, and give them surprising powers of communication.

On the other hand, something like *the community are technology enthusiasts* jars: it's difficult to justify the claim that the community is acting as separate individuals. I'd have gone for *the community consists*

FAQ – The media are?
The data indicate?

Media and *data* are Latin plurals (the singulars being *medium* and *datum*), but the terms *the media* and *the mass media* – meaning newspapers, radio, TV, etc., as a way of communicating information – have been used as if they were singular for almost a hundred years: the OED quotes one G. Snow in a publication called *Advertising and Selling* as saying, way back in 1923, 'Mass media *represents* the most economical way of getting the story over the new and wider market in the least time.' The word's origins have been so sweepingly forgotten that you even see reference to *a media* or *various medias*. I confess that both of those make me cringe a little, but *the media is* has achieved such general currency that only the truly masochistic continue to bang their heads against the wall about it.

Data, similarly, is strictly-speaking-a-plural-widely-used-as-a-singular. Scientists often still write meticulously *the data show . . .*, perhaps because they see themselves as putting one piece of datum together with another to produce a result. Most of the rest of us, frankly, don't bother, and some of us even say *datas* when we want a plural (though I am cringing again here).

Following on from data and media, we find *bacteria,* another plural whose singular form ends in

–um. Latin again. As is *symposium*, whose plural is *symposia*, and *curriculum*, plural *curricula.* If for some reason you need to write two CVs, the plural is *curricula vitae* (the *vitae* bit means 'of life' and therefore doesn't need to be changed). If several people were writing their CVs, there'd be a school of thought that wanted to call them *curricula vitarum*, but let's not go there.

Some Latin-derived words whose singulars end in *–us* have plurals ending in *–i*, such as *alumni*, *cacti*, *termini*, *uteri*, and one or two that end in *–a* form plurals with *–ae*: *alumnae* (the feminine form of *alumni*), *formulae.*

An *addendum* is a (single) thing to be added, so its plural is *addenda.* But an *agenda* is a list of a number of things to be done; once upon a time it was treated as plural but is now regarded as singular. If you happen to be preparing for more than one meeting, the plural is *agendas* – not *agendae* or (please) *agenda's.*

Graffiti is an Italian plural, but all but the purest of the pure use it as a singular in English: *the graffiti on the toilet wall* are *very funny* just doesn't sound right. If this bothers you, pretend you are exercising discernment as well as precise syntax and say *some of the graffiti is very funny* instead.

of or *is made up of technology enthusiasts* or *all the members of the community are...*

And on yet another hand, the issue has been around for some time. The opening credits of Alfred Hitchcock's 1946 film *Notorious* announce that *RKO Pictures. Inc. presents ...* The odd use of full stops notwithstanding, it's clear that RKO Pictures was deemed to be a company whose employees all pulled together as one.

Whichever version you opt for, stick with it. Even the great Sir David Attenborough got it wrong when, filming on the Great Barrier Reef, he announced that, after a gap between shoots, *The team returns to see if their plan is working.* This breaks the unbreakable editorial rule: 'If you can't be right, be consistent.' Either the team is a single entity, in which case it *returns* to see if *its* plan is working; or it's a group of individuals who *return* to see if *their* plan is working.

If you're uncomfortable with this, slot in the words 'members of the [team, jury, board of directors]'. This removes any shadow of doubt: plural subject, plural verb, next question please.

And the winner are . . .

Plural verbs following the name of a team are a sort of spin-off from this. They may or may not be 'correct', but they are so well established that they barely

A macédoine?

A certain frozen-food specialist has come up with a new singular: *veg*. Although the packet illustrated in their catalogue is labelled 'Mixed Vegetables' – clearly plural – the copy next to it reads *Mixed veg* offers *so much for so little*. I'm not sure I approve of that, despite the claims being made for the vegetables' nutritional value, but perhaps the company could make a case for mixed veg acting as a single entity.

raise an eyebrow and can even resolve ambiguities. A sentence such as *Leicester* are *welcoming many more visitors since they moved to their new stadium* is clearly about the football team; *Leicester* is *welcoming many more visitors since the Foxes moved to the new stadium* means that the city itself is benefiting.

During the same sporting season, a commentator on the rugby Six Nations tournament, advising us one Friday night of the treats in store over the weekend, announced that *Scotland* is *in Rome tomorrow*. It sounded as if the almost-independent nation was going to raise the flag of St Andrew in the Colosseum, rather than sending fifteen players to the Stadio Olimpico to take on the Italian team. Interestingly, the commentator was using the present tense to create a sense of excitement: had he stuck to the more logical future tense (*Scotland* will be *in Rome tomorrow*), the issue wouldn't have arisen.

Another spin-off: English has a number of confusing 'sound like plural, behave like singular' nouns: games whose name ends in *s* (*dominoes*, *billiards*, *darts*) are treated as singular, as are diseases such as *measles* and *mumps* and academic disciplines such as *mathematics*, *economics* and *statistics*. But very few things in English are that simple: in the last case, singular verbs are used only when you are considering the nouns as single entities: *Economics* was *my favourite subject at school* or *Statistics* was *the hardest part of my maths course*. But treat these terms as something more countable, something made up of individual components and you (correctly) arrive at *The economics of the decision* are *far from straightforward* or *Statistics can prove anything if you know how to manipulate* them.

Other things that 'sound' plural but are grammatically singular include names of books, films, works of art and the like:

Pride and Prejudice is *my favourite book* (but *pride and prejudice* are *unpleasant character traits*).

Close Encounters *was the first film I ever saw* (but *close encounters* are *often reported in ufology magazines*).

Van Gogh's Sunflowers is *on display in the National Gallery* (but *the sunflowers in my garden* are *glorious this year*).

FAQ – What's the difference between less and fewer?

It's to do with what are called *countable* and *uncountable* (or *mass*) nouns. A countable noun denotes something you can count: *one banana*, *two oranges*, *six eggs*. An uncountable noun denotes something you have 'some' of: *bread*, *butter*, *washing-up liquid*. You might have *three loaves of bread*, but you are counting the loaves; you don't have *three breads*.

If you want a larger number or quantity of any of these items, countable or otherwise, you use *more* – *more oranges*, *more washing-up liquid*. But if you want a smaller number or quantity? Aha. There, as they say, is the rub.

If you want a smaller *number*, use *fewer*. For a smaller *quantity*, use *less*. *Fewer oranges*, *less washing-up liquid*.

How do you remember this? If you can have *a few of* something, you have *fewer* of them: you could buy *a few bananas*; if you had too many, you could buy *fewer* next time. But you can't buy *a few butters*, so next time you would buy *less*.

Me, myself and I

When I was promoting the book *My Grammar and I (or should that be 'Me'?)* some years ago, I was often asked, 'Well, which is it?' The person asking the question wasn't always entirely happy when I said, 'It depends', but that is the honest answer.

Whether you use *I* or *me* depends on whether it is the subject or the object of the verb. *I* is the subject form, *me* is the object. It's difficult to come up with many plausible sentences using 'my grammar and I/me', so let's change it to *grandma*, just for the moment:

My grandma and I are very fond of cream cakes (I *is part of the subject of the verb*).
Everybody likes my grandma and me (me *is part of the object*).

You also use the object form after a preposition:

No one spoke to my grandma and me.

If in doubt in sentences such as this, take out *my grandma and* (or its equivalent) and see what you're left with:

I (not *me*) *am very fond of cream cakes.*
Everybody likes me (not *I*).
No one spoke to me (not *I*).

The same applies with *he/him, she/her, we/us* and

they/them: the first of each pair is the subject, the second is the object.

His grandma and he (or *he and his grandma*) *often went to the match together.*
Everyone stared at his grandma and him.

She and her grandma were the best of friends.
Going out together was fun for her grandma and her.

We and our grandma have lots in common.

Hmm. It's getting a bit forced now, but you get the idea.

Before we leave the subject of grandmas, the expression 'Let's eat, Grandma' is frequently used to indicate the importance of commas. (Omit that particular comma and what is left means something else entirely.) So widespread has it become that two teenage girls from Norwich chose it – without the comma – as the name for their psychedelic pop band, which apparently aims at being as weird as possible and getting people to take the recorder seriously. Who'd have thought that a joke based on punctuation could have such far-reaching effects? One reviewer referred to the band as 'alarmingly named', suggesting that the joke hadn't quite reached him.

Moving on. We come to the vexed question of *myself*. And *yourself*, *himself*, *ourselves* and the rest of them. These are either reflexive pronouns:

Don't answer the question for me: I can speak for myself.

You should have looked at yourself in a mirror before you went out dressed like that.

He is old enough to behave himself in a restaurant.

Or they are emphatic pronouns:

The Northern Lights were often visible nearby, but he himself had never seen them.

I want you all to do your homework yourselves. Don't copy from each other.

They went to the office themselves: they didn't trust the courier to act for them.

What these words are *not* is substitutes for *I/me, you, he/him* or any other of the personal pronouns. If a salesperson tells you that a handbag may be *just what yourself is looking for*, you're allowed to be tempted to slosh him with it. He means *just what* you *are looking for* and the *–self* adds absolutely nothing. If a flight attendant bringing round the duty free announces 'We've got a great range of products for yourselves today', curb the violence: it's frowned upon on aircraft. And there is no need to say things like, 'Alex and myself are going on holiday together.' *Alex and I* is what you want.

I suspect that this particular nonsense has arisen because people are afraid of getting *I* and *me* confused.

There's no need. Learn the simple distinction explained here and then you can happily stick to using *myself* for emphasis when you need it.

Some people may also think *myself*, *yourself* and so forth sound more upmarket or more intelligent than the shorter alternatives. They're mistaken.

If we must, we must

A friend surprised me by saying that he'd come to loathe the word *we*. When I asked him why, he pointed out that his wife saying, '*We* must get the spare bedroom redecorated' meant '*I* want *you* to redecorate the spare bedroom', while a politician announcing that *we* must cut down on carbon emissions means that *you* must buy a more eco-friendly car. I suspect that my friend was making a domestic and political point rather than a grammatical one, but it's a neat example of the way meanings can be twisted.

Dangling participles

The narrator of a documentary on seabirds remarked of the skua, 'Nesting on the ground away from the shore, I've always admired its utter fearlessness in defence of its territory.'

You know what he means, you may well share his admiration for the bird's fearlessness, but grammatically what he has *said* is that he, the narrator, not the skua, is nesting on the ground.

The rule that has been broken here is that the participial phrase (the bit beginning with the participle 'nesting') should have the same subject as the main clause. You have to rejig to produce something like 'Nesting on the ground away from the shore, the skua shows utter fearlessness in defence of its territory. I've always admired that' or 'Watching it nest on the ground away from the shore, I've always admired its utter fearlessness in defence of its territory.' It's interesting – and doubtless significant – to note that neither of my 'correct' versions has the dramatic impact of the original. Which is probably why the writer chose to write what he did, and one of the reasons this sort of construction – known as a dangling or misrelated participle or modifier – is gaining ground.

Another, more complicated example, this time from a modern novel. A character waiting to be summoned to a meeting watches a fly buzzing round and round the reception area in a repeating pattern:

Neither food, nor water, nor searching for other flies appeared to be on its mind, preferring instead to remain trapped in a world of its own making.

In this instance the subject of the main verb *appeared* is the rather lengthy noun phrase *Neither food, nor water, nor searching for other flies.* The subject of the participial phrase *preferring instead . . .* is the fly. There is no obvious way to make *Neither food, nor water*, etc. the subject of the rest of the sentence, so there are two options. Either

- make the fly the subject of the main clause: *It appeared to have neither food, nor water, nor searching for other flies on its mind, preferring instead to remain trapped in a world of its own making.*

  or

- make cunning use of a semicolon and turn the subsidiary phrase into a clause, with its own finite verb (which can then have any subject you care to give it): *Neither food, nor water, nor searching for other flies appeared to be on its mind; it preferred instead to remain trapped in a world of its own making.*

More straightforward (and easily remedied) instances of dangling or misrelated participles are along the lines of:

Walking down the road, the shops seemed even scruffier than she remembered.

Grammatically, this says that the shops are walking down the road – which presumably isn't the case. Again, you need to rejig either so that both parts of the sentence have the same subject . . .

Walking down the road, she was struck by the scruffiness of the shops – she hadn't remembered they were as bad as this.

. . . or so that the subsidiary clause has a clearly expressed subject of its own:

As she walked down the road, the shops seemed even scruffier than she remembered.

FAQ – What's a participial phrase?

The phrases in these examples are called participial because they contain participles. There are two sorts of participles – present, which ends in *–ing* and is used in the continuous present tense (*I am walking, you are talking, we are having fun*) and past, which with regular verbs ends in *–ed* and occurs in finite verbs such as *I had walked, you should have hurried, he hasn't answered my letter.* There are lots of irregular past participles – *I had* been, *you haven't* forgotten, *he has* gone, *they have* done *the deed* – but they all serve the same grammatical purpose. Combined with an auxiliary verb (*am, are, have, may, will* and so forth) they form a finite verb.

FAQ – Remind me: what's an auxiliary verb?

Auxiliary means 'helping, supporting' and an *auxiliary verb* is used to indicate tense, mood, voice, etc. when these are not made clear by the *inflection* or change of ending.

So all the words listed in the previous FAQ – *am*, *are*, *have*, *may*, *will* – and many others, including *do*, *could*, *would*, *should* – combine with participles or infinitives to form finite verbs:

I am going to be late.
We are setting off after breakfast.
They have done their homework.
I may spend the night at Jill's place.
I will write to her tomorrow.
They do worry about you.
You could go by train.
They would love to be invited.
We should book our holiday soon.

Some tenses require more than one auxiliary verb, one of which is a form of *have*:

I should have known that would happen.
We would have come earlier if we'd known – it wouldn't have been inconvenient.
They might have asked permission before they borrowed the car.
It must have been after midnight when they came home.

Have in these sentences is often shortened to *'ve*: *I should've known*, *we would've come* and so on. And this has led to one of the most widespread of all English errors: replacing this *'ve* with *of*. But there is no grammatical justification for *I should of*, *we would of*. *Of* is a preposition used in expressions from *a packet of sweets* to *a will of iron*, *the city of Athens* to *a knowledge of philosophy*. And it is never anything other than a preposition. It's certainly never an auxiliary verb.

It's easy to get away with saying *should of* because it sounds so like *should've*. But writing it is a real howler.

CHAPTER 4

Taking the rough with the thorough

Why English is so difficult – spelling and confusable words

We hear a lot about the illogicality of English spelling – the many pronunciations of *ough*, for example (*borough*, *bough*, *brought*, *cough*, *dough*, *rough*, to name but six); the silent letters in *castle*, *gnome*, *psychology* and *thumb*; and the fact that *mint* doesn't rhyme with *pint* while *main* rhymes with both *rein* and *reign* and *row* can rhyme with either *cow* or *show*, depending on whether you are having an argument or competing in a boat race. It makes English a joy for lovers of puns and crosswords and something of an ordeal for foreigners.

There's more: *bomb*, *comb* and *tomb* don't rhyme, *do* and *don't*, *can* and *can't* have different vowel sounds, and if you cut something in two you *bisect* it (with one *s*), but if you cut it open and take it apart bit by bit you *dissect* it (with two).

Particularly difficult for foreigners must be the name of the Scottish bird the *ptarmigan*. It comes from Scottish Gaelic and should logically begin with a *t*; the silent *p* seems to have arisen through analogy or confusion with the Greek-based prefix *ptero–*, which means wing, and is familiar to most of us thanks to that rather older birdlike creature, the *pterodactyl*.

Words ending in *–able* or *–ible*, *–ant* or *–ent*, *–ance or –ence* are a minefield. Why should we write *abominable* but *admissible*, *changeable* but *convertible*, *extravagant* but *excellent*? A thorough knowledge of Latin will help you a bit, but even then there are exceptions and there is little the non-scholar can do but learn them by heart. Once you've learned a word, though, you may well find you have learned two or three, because *extravagance* follows the same pattern as *extravagant* while *excellence* and *excellency* tally with *excellent*, and so on, with almost all words of this type.

One (further) oddity: *independent* is spelled with an *e*, as is the adjective *dependent*; you might be *dependent* on morphine, or on your rich uncle to pay you an allowance. If the former, you suffer from a *dependency*; if the latter, you are one of your uncle's *dependants*.

e or no e?

Words such as *changeable, knowledgeable and noticeable* – derived, obviously, from *change, knowledge* and *notice* – retain the *e* after the *g* and *c*, whereas lots of other words ending in *e* drop that letter when you add a suffix: *admirable, conceivable, debatable* – and *admiring, conceiving, debating*, not to mention *chasing, dilettantism, purplish, wastage* and many more.

The reason *changeable* and the others retain the *e* is that *c* and *g* can be pronounced in two different ways, depending on the vowel that follows them. A *c* followed by *a, o* or *u* is a hard, *k* sound – as in *catastrophe, collision, cumbersome*; followed by an *e* or an *i* it is a soft, *s* sound – *cereal, cinnamon*. With a *g* the same idea applies: here the difference is between the hard *garland, goldfish, gullible* and the soft, *j* sound of *gentleman* or *gibberish*.

This isn't a rule so much as a guideline, and the soft sounds tend to appear in words that derive from Latin and/or French. Simple, everyday words such as *girl* and *get* often come from Anglo-Saxon and other northern European ancestors where the harder sounds predominate.

To preserve the soft sounds of *manage* and *notice*, therefore, we retain the *e* in *manageable* and *noticeable*: it isn't pronounced, it simply influences the consonant that precedes it. We also have a handful of words such as *panicking* and *picnicking* where we cunningly insert a *k* (always pronounced in the same way) to preserve the hard sound of the less single-minded *c*. The silent *u* in *guest*, *guide* and *harangue* (not to mention more

---

A mischievous little word

The ending *–ous* means 'full of, characterized by, of the nature of' whatever quality is embodied in the word it is tacked on to. *Beauteous* = full of beauty; *cautious* = characterized by caution; *courteous*, *dangerous*, *glorious*, *infamous*, *nauseous*, *spacious* – the list is a long one. Very often, in order to produce these adjectives, you have to knock something off the end of the related nouns: the *y* of *beauty*, *glory* and *infamy*, the *sy* of *courtesy*, the *a* of *nausea*, the *e* of *space*. If the noun ends in an *f*, however, you change it to a *v*, giving *grievous* rather than *griefous* and *mischievous* rather than *mischiefous*.

Which brings me to the point of this little section: *mischievous* is derived from *mischief*. Note the *ie* before the *v* and the *f*. Those vowels stay where they are, and the emphasis is on the first syllable. Contrary to what many, many people believe, there is no such word as *mischevious*.

---

obviously foreign words such as *guerrilla*) is there to harden the *g*.

Sometimes we retain the *e* not for reasons of pronunciation but to avoid ambiguity: *milage* and *salable* might be logical spellings – and are the norm in American English – but to many British eyes they are odd: might they mean something to do with mills and salt? We break the rules (or the norms) in order to make ourselves clear and use *mileage* for the number of miles we have covered and *saleable* for an article that we might consider buying.

Double consonants

Benefited or *benefitted*? *Traveler* or *traveller*? There is a rule, but it's a weird one. If the infinitive of a word *ending in a single consonant preceded by a single vowel* is stressed on its last syllable, you double the consonant when adding an ending such as *–ed*, *–er* or *–ing*. If the stress falls earlier in the word, the single consonant remains:

> *admit*, *admitted*, *admitting*
> *confer*, *conferred*, *conferring* (but *conference* – these rules don't always apply to nouns and adjectives derived from the verbs)
> *develop*, *developed*, *developing*, *development*

focus, *focused*, *focusing* (though the American doubling of the *s* has drifted across the Atlantic and is frequently seen)

In the British spelling of a word ending in a single vowel followed by a single *l*, the *l* is always doubled:

compelled, *traveller*, *unravelling*

If the word ends in two consonants or in two vowels followed by a consonant, there's no doubling:

faint, fainted, fainting
track, tracked, tracking, tracker
want, wanted, wanting

forfeit, forfeited, forfeiting
heal, healed, healing, healer
tweet, tweeted, tweeting

And for the purposes of this rule, the *u* that follows a *q* doesn't count as a vowel:

quiz, quizzed, quizzing

Bear in mind, too, that we have lots of words that are stressed differently according to what part of speech they are. Thus a *reb*el (with or without a cause) may re*bel* against something and would be said to have *rebelled* (in, as it happens, a *rebellion*).

As for *accommodate, broccoli, cemetery, dissipation, extrovert, frieze, guarantee, hypocrisy, idiosyncrasy, jewellery, kaleidoscope, liaison, mantelpiece, naphthalene, obsequious, parallelogram, quandary, rarefy, sacrilege, teetotaller, umbelliferous, vacuum, wilful, xenophobic, yashmak* and *ziggurat,* you just have to get used to them.

FAQ – Burned or burnt?
Learned or learnt?

Not to mention *leaned or leant*? *Spelled or spelt*? *Spoiled or spoilt*? For the past tense and past participle of the verbs (*I burned, I have burned*), both are acceptable in British English, *burned, learned*, etc. being more usual in American. Both sides of the Atlantic prefer the *–t* form for adjectives (*the burnt papers, a spoilt child*), though *a learned speech* (pronounced as two syllables and meaning an erudite one) would differ from *a learnt one* (one you had learned by heart).

Whether you go for *leaned* or *leant*, remember that these are to do with leaning. *Lent* is the past form of *lend* or *loan.* Which, while we're here, is not the same thing as *borrowing.* You *lend* someone money (and expect them to give it back sometime); they *borrow* it from you.

It literally drives me insane

The (mis)use of *literally* has been driving grammar pundits figuratively insane for a long time, but never more so than since that sad day in 2013 when several respected dictionaries conceded that it was 'used for emphasis while not being literally true'. That very definition makes the purists (and I admit to being one of them here) tear their hair out: how can *literally* mean something that *isn't literally true*?

What it *really* means is 'according to the letter, absolutely truly, not metaphorically or figuratively'. Something that *literally* drives you insane might put you in an institution for your own protection, or at the centre of a horror story with your hair standing on end. Something that metaphorically drives you insane just makes you very angry. It could be your partner's failure to empty the dishwasher, or the fact that your bus always seems to be late when it rains. I think you'll agree that there is a difference.

Using the wrong words

My local newspaper reports, approvingly, a scheme for providing careers education to young people who are still at school. The Work and Pensions Secretary, it says, 'threatens to send Job Centre Staff into the classrooms to deliver good careers advice'.

Good for him, you may say, but we aren't going into the politics here. My issue is with the use of the word *threatens*. A *threat* is 'a declaration of the intention to inflict harm, pain or misery; an indication of imminent harm, danger or pain'. *To threaten* is 'to be or to express a threat to'. So the Work and Pensions Secretary might have *threatened* to close down Job Centres or to fine schools that didn't provide careers advice; as it is, in announcing his thoughts on sending Job Centre Staff into classrooms for benevolent purposes, he should be described as *suggesting* or *proposing* or perhaps – if the idea was in his party's manifesto – *promising*.

The point is that this misuse of a word weakens it and, if it becomes widespread, means you have to find a new word for the original sense. If you can *threaten* to send Job Centre staff into classrooms, isn't it a bit feeble to talk about the *threat* of global warming or of international terrorism? Will they have to become *menaces*? Or should we revive a word that is in the dictionaries but not on the tip of most of our tongues: *commination*, say, or *anathematization*?

The American poet and physician Oliver Wendell Holmes, writing in the mid-nineteenth century, called this practice *verbicide*: in his wonderfully named *The Autocrat of the Breakfast Table*, he wrote (autocratically), 'Homicide and *verbicide* – that is, violent treatment of a word with fatal results to its legitimate meaning – are alike forbidden.'

Shame is another example, much loved by the writers of sports headlines. A player is said to be *keen to put last week's shame behind him.* To me, that headline suggests that he cheated, became violent, was sent off and was possibly caught with a colleague's wife before the match was over. But no: his team was beaten soundly. An embarrassment, certainly, or, to quote the same player in the same report, *a shock to the system and a wake-up call* – but is it really shameful?

We do much the same thing with *legend*, which does still mean 'a story or body of stories, handed down through the generations but not historically verified' as in *the legend of King Arthur*, but now also describes a famous person who's been around for a long time. Is Donny Osmond really legendary? An advertisement on my local radio station has just said so.

On the other hand, a recent television documentary referred to *mythical cities* such as Samarkand. A nit-pick: *mythical* suggests that they didn't exist or that they involved interactions between mortals and gods or other supernatural beings. Samarkand did exist – still does; it's one of the oldest inhabited cities in the world and thanks to its exotic history it comes close to justifying the epithet *legendary*.

We've done the same thing (and there is no going back on it now) with *awful* and *awesome*. The prolific hymn-writer Isaac Watts came up with this warning:

Before Jehovah's awful throne,
Ye nations, bow with sacred joy;
Know that the Lord is God alone;
He can create, and He destroy.

That was in the early eighteenth century and I'm sure schoolchildren then didn't giggle the way we did when we sang it. Jehovah – God – wouldn't have had an awful throne in the modern sense: he'd have had a pretty smart, rich, gold-laden one, we thought. But Watts didn't mean that: he meant *full of awe*: awe-inspiring, something well worth bowing down in front of. As for *abysmal*, there was a time when it applied to the depths of Hell or to anything else dark and bottomless, not just to a government's record on health care or a car's disappointing performance.

Mind you, this isn't a new phenomenon and it is one of the natural ways in which language changes. When Shakespeare wrote:

How far that little candle throws his beams!
So shines a good deed in a naughty world

he meant that the world was morally bad, wicked, not mildly mischievous or disobedient. He would also have been aware of *naughty* meaning promiscuous or sexually disreputable, but he'd have found it hard to imagine that 400 years later we would be calling children who pulled their sister's pigtails naughty.

And, while we are talking about the sexually disreputable, did Dickens realize what an odd double entendre he was creating when he wrote (in *David Copperfield*), *There was an interval of silence, only broken by Miss Betsey's occasionally ejaculating 'Ha!' as she sat with her feet upon the fender*?

An obstacle illusion

The journalistic habit of debasing a powerful word by using it in a trivial context is just one aspect of the wrong word in the wrong place. A couple of years ago, under the heading *Acyrologia*, American Mensa published a piece that began with a definition of its title:

> *An incorrect use of words – particulately replacing one word with another word that sounds similar but has a diffident meaning – possibly fuelled by a deep-seeded desire to sound more educated.*

There is plenty more in the same vein: in a paragraph of about 180 words, the authors manage to introduce over twenty acyrological examples, including *people of that elk*, *post-dramatic stress disorder* and, my favourite, *curled up in the feeble position.*

Mistakes of this kind are more often called *malapropisms*, after a character in Richard Brinsley Sheridan's eighteenth-century play *The Rivals*. Mrs

Malaprop litters her speech with words used *mal à propos* – 'at the wrong moment'. She tells her niece Lydia to forget about an impoverished suitor: 'Illiterate him, I say, quite from your memory', and when Lydia objects, describes her as 'a little intricate hussy'. She had sent Lydia to school to acquire 'a supercilious knowledge in accounts' and to be 'instructed in geometry, that she might know something of the contagious countries'. In short, poor Mrs Malaprop can't open her mouth without making herself sound ridiculous or, as she would put it, 'If I reprehend any thing in this world, it is the use of my oracular tongue, and a nice derangement of epitaphs!'

One of the reasons this sort of thing happens is that too many of us, like Mrs Malaprop herself, are frightened of using an ordinary word when there is a fancy one available: we seem to think it will make us sound – well, ordinary. But – IMHO – it's better to be ordinary and accurate than to try to sound clever or sophisticated and get it wrong.

A case in point: the caption to a photo of Sir John Betjeman told me that the late Poet Laureate was 'an unavowed populist'. I hesitate to contradict the curators of a major London gallery, but *to avow* means to admit openly, so to be *unavowed* is to be secretive, in this instance a 'closet' populist. Betjeman, in fact, was an *unabashed* populist, a frankly open and acknowledged populist – an *avowed* one, in other words. This isn't, to my mind, a case of confusing one word with another; it's trying to say something that sounds good without going to the trouble of finding out what the words you are using mean.

There is no alternate

English is, of course, riddled with words that sound sufficiently similar to be easily confused.

Let's take, for example, *alternate* and *alternative*. *Alternate* as a verb means to take it in turns – *they alternated shifts: he worked on Mondays, Wednesdays and Fridays and she did Tuesdays, Thursdays and Saturdays* – or to swing from one thing to another: *he alternated between great happiness and the depths of despair.* As an adjective, it means occurring by turns: *alternate moments of enthusiasm and misery. Alternative*, as an adjective or a noun, offers a choice: *this road is closed – please seek an alternative route* or *you have no alternative – you must do what he says.*

In British English, to say *please seek an alternate route* is wrong, though it has been accepted in American English for many years: when Mickey Dolenz of 1960s boy band The Monkees wrote a song whose title was considered rude, he was asked to come up with an *alternate* title and 'Alternate Title' remains the song's name to this day.

Purists will tell you that – because of the meaning

of the word's Latin source – an *alternative* is a choice between two things only; with more than two you have a *choice* or *various options*. But this is being very pure indeed.

Confusable words

Alternate/alternative is only one of scores of pairs that are easy to confuse but worth differentiating if you want to express yourself with precision. Here are some more:

- I am sending you *advance* notification – the takeover will not be announced until the end of the week. But discussions are well *advanced*: the deal is certain to go ahead.

- I will *apprise* (= advise) you of our decision when we have *appraised* (= assessed) the financial position.

- I'm not *averse* to going to the Bahamas, providing there are no *adverse* weather warnings.

- My idea that they had enjoyed their Easter holidays was *borne* out when their baby was *born* on Christmas Day.

- I can't *bear* that woman: she is such a *bare*faced liar.

- This is the *definitive* guide to Paris: it tells you everything you could possibly need to know. I will *definitely* take it with me when I go next week.

My compliments to . . .

Things that *complement* each other make a whole out of individual parts or simply go well together: *the handbag complemented her dress and shoes.* A popular cruise ship may set sail with a full *complement* of passengers; *complementary* medicine is taken alongside conventional treatment.

A *compliment*, on the other hand, is a pleasant remark or a commendation: *allow me to compliment you on your success.* If you were to be given a *complimentary* ticket to a concert – meaning that you didn't have to pay to get in, you were given it with the *compliments* of the management – it would be spelled this way.

And here's a crafty ambiguity, from a flyer advertising *prestige* (as opposed to *prestigious*) hire cars: the company's mission statement is *to compliment one's lifestyle, offering a polite and reliable service ...* I'm sure they meant *to complement one's lifestyle*, but the assurance of politeness suggests they might make *paying compliments* part of the service too.

- His salary increase was so *derisory* that he greeted it with a *derisive* snort.

- I always feel a bit *diffident* introducing myself to strangers. I expect them to think I am a Soviet *dissident.*

- The gym where the celebrities work out is in a *discrete* part of the hotel – you have to cross the courtyard to get to it. The manager is very *discreet*, and never boasts about who is staying there.

- 'I expect it will rain all summer,' he said *dully*. And he was right – it *duly* did.

- The *eminent* academic threw a party when his departure to Harvard was *imminent*.

- There's nothing *exceptionable* about her promotion – I don't see why you should object to it when she has done such *exceptional* work.

- The boxer *feinted* to his right when he saw a *faint* chance of getting through his opponent's guard.

- If you keep *floundering* about and not getting on with the job, the deadline will pass, the funds will run out and the project will *founder*.

- Prince was still dubbed 'the artist *formerly* known as Prince' when he was *formally* inducted into the Rock and Roll Hall of Fame.

- The man is a *genius*: he keeps coming up with *ingenious* ways of solving our problems.

- His handwriting is completely *illegible* – I can't read a word of it. Even if I could, his thoughts are so muddled that his report would probably be

Before you go

A useful rule of thumb: words beginning *fore–* are likely to have something to do with going *before*.

Thus a *foreword* is an introductory section in a book – the words that go *before* the main body of the text. *Forward* is the spelling for most other meanings: *to step forward, a forward pass, a forward* (cheeky) *remark.*

A *forebear* is an ancestor, someone who lived *before* you. *To forbear* is to refrain from doing something: *I will forbear from punishing you this time, but don't let it happen again.*

To forego is a rarely used word meaning 'to go before'; its past participle *foregone* often appears in the phrase *a foregone conclusion*, an inevitable one, one that has already been made. *Forgo* comes from an Old English word meaning 'to do without' and is the spelling you want in expressions such as *I shall have to forgo the pleasure of attending the conference.*

There is no such word as the recently spotted *fourth-coming. Forthcoming* (as in *the forthcoming meeting* – the one scheduled for next week), *forthright, forthwith, henceforth* and its synonym *henceforward* are all related to *fore–* and *forward*. A *fourth coming* has bizarre Christian overtones, as if Christ's Second Coming (and presumably his third) had somehow gone awry.

unintelligible. There is no way he is *eligible* for a place on the board.

- I'm *incredulous* that you should believe such an *incredible* story.

- I'm *loath* (or *loth*) to do a favour for someone I *loathe*.

- Don't let me *loose* in the casino – I can't afford to *lose* any more money.

- It was a *masterly* piece of acting. I couldn't believe that someone who was so *masterful* in private life could play such a gentle character.

- You had better be on your *mettle*: the woman from the Goldsmiths' Hall knows more about precious *metals* than any of us.

- A *momentary* silence greeted the announcement; then applause broke out as the audience recognized what *momentous* news it was.

- The *moral* of the story is that poor food and harsh discipline were bad for the troops' *morale*.

- The *official* position was that the treasurer could deal with the matter on his own, but one *officious* member of the committee kept offering unwanted help.

- The *principal* violinist always insisted on the best dressing-room: it was, he said, a matter of *principle*.

- The King kept the Crown Prince on a tight *rein* – he didn't want any nonsense during his *reign*.

- We wanted to see all the *sights*, but there was so much renovation going on at the palace that it looked like a building *site*.

- The conjuror's movements were so *slight* that no one in the audience realized what was going on – he fooled them with his *sleight* of hand.

- He *straightened* his tie and tidied his hair: his *straitened* circumstances were no excuse for looking scruffy.

- The *two* of us have decided not to go to a bar: it'll be *too* noisy. We are going for a pizza. Would you like to come *too*?

- I *wonder* if it is going to be fine tomorrow; it would be lovely to *wander* in the countryside if it is.

And here's a handful of words that strictly speaking don't mean what you probably think they do:

anticipate is so often used to mean 'expect' that the purists are fighting a losing battle. But they still insist that it should be reserved for situations in which you realize something is going to happen and take appropriate action: *He anticipated the fall in property prices by selling his country house.* If we are being picky,

I don't anticipate any problems – I'm sure the deal will go through or *He didn't anticipate her reaction – it took him completely by surprise* should, as the dictionaries say, be avoided by careful users of English.

chronic derives from the Greek for time and, used of a disease, means long-lasting. It isn't necessarily serious: you might suffer from *chronic catarrh*, which would be irritating but not life-threatening. The opposite of this is an *acute* illness, which flares up quickly and with any luck goes away again with much the same speed.

crescendo means growing. So in music a *crescendo* is a passage that starts softly and grows louder. It may then reach a climax. Saying *to reach a crescendo* when you mean to reach a peak, to become very loud, will annoy the musicians of your acquaintance.

decimate is another one for nit-pickers only. Back in the day, it was a Roman punishment, killing one man in ten until the genuine wrongdoer confessed. If you were writing about Roman history, you might still have occasion to use it in this sense. In modern life, thank goodness, this doesn't crop up very often, but purists still insist on the 'one in ten' aspect of the word. Very few people who say *The hurricane decimated the island* mean that 10 per cent of the island has been destroyed; they'd be indicating that most of it had been ravaged and the dictionaries acknowledge this fact. But if you want to avoid offending those touchy people we keep coming up against in this book, avoid the issue by using the perfectly acceptable and equally powerful *devastated* instead.

enormity is nothing to do with size. It's to do with wickedness: *Only when he saw her lifeless body did he realize the enormity of what he had done.* There is a word *enormousness*, but it's perhaps a bit of a mouthful – if you want to convey great size, try *hugeness*, *immensity* or *vastness*.

fulsome is not a compliment. *Fulsome praise* is over the top, gushing and not likely to be sincere. If you want to describe praise that is at just the right level and that you are pleased to receive, you could opt for *enthusiastic*, *fervent* or *generous.*

fortuitous means happening by chance, which may be good or bad. *Your winning the Nobel Prize was fortuitous* means that it happened out of the blue; if it also enhanced your career and made it easier for you to attract funding, it was *fortunate.*

momentarily is a word that American English happily uses to mean 'in a moment': *don't hassle me, I'll do it momentarily.* British English would prefer *I'll do it in a moment*, leaving *momentarily* to mean '*for* a moment': *he paused momentarily at the end of the diving board before plunging into the pool.*

Your Winning Ways

If you're wondering why I wrote *your winning* in the entry for 'fortuitous' rather than *you winning*, let me explain. *Winning* in this sentence is what's called a verbal noun: it looks like part of a verb but is functioning as a noun. So it needs the possessive adjective *your*. Change *winning* to something that looks like a noun and you'll see the point: you'd say *your grasp on the Nobel Prize* rather than *you grasp*, wouldn't you? Again, it isn't something that crops up very often, but it's good to know for formal occasions.

revert means to go back to something you used to do (*She reverted to her old bad habits whenever he wasn't looking*) or to a subject that was previously under discussion (*To revert to the subject of wedding plans, what are we going to do about Aunt Maud?*). Using it to mean *reply*, *get back to you* (*I'll revert as soon as I've read the contract*) is surely both ugly and unnecessary.

And while we're being pedantic . . .

There's also a useful distinction to be made between:

- **continuous** and **continual:** the first means 'non-stop', the second 'over and over again, with intervals in between'. So you might be annoyed equally by

A genteel reminder

Then we have shades of meaning, as in the difference between *cleaning* and *cleansing*. *Cleaning* is about – well, getting things clean. You do it to the kitchen work surfaces. You wouldn't clean your face, or clean your mind of impure thoughts: both of those would be *cleansing*. There's something about it that is more personal, more deep-rooted and more ritualistic.

Gentle and *genteel* have the same derivation and both once meant graceful and refined in manners, having the qualities of a *gentleman* or *gentlewoman*. But the two words have drifted apart. *Gentle* has come to mean mild, soothing or gradual (*a gentle word*, *a gentle pat*, *a gentle slope*), while genteel has acquired a disparaging note and now tends to mean *falsely* refined.

your daughter's *continually* (day after day after day) forgetting her homework and by her *continuous* loud music (which she never stops playing).

- **disinterested** and **uninterested:** *Uninterested* means having no interest in, bored by; *disinterested* means having no interest in – for example – an outcome or a verdict, in the sense of having nothing to gain from it, impartial. So, although *disinterested* is often used nowadays as if it meant *uninterested*

('I'm completely disinterested in tennis'), I'd still prefer to have a disinterested judge and jury if ever I am on trial for my life. This 'error', by the way, has a formidable poetic pedigree: Rebecca Gowers in *Horrible Words* points out that John Donne in 1631 uses 'disinterested' to mean 'unconcerned'; William Cowper in 1767 has 'uninterested' meaning 'impartial'. I stick to my opinion, however: there are two clearly defined meanings here, and we conveniently have two words with which to express them, so why not hang on to the distinction?

- **imply** and **infer:** to *imply* something is to suggest it without saying it in so many words; to *infer* is to deduce something that hasn't actually been said. For example, 'Are you *implying* that I'm a liar?' 'I'm *implying* nothing. What you choose to *infer* is up to you.'

And finally, a friend was describing her daughter's eclectic taste in clothes: 'She loves little black dresses with pearls, vintage flowery prints, the whole gambit,' she said. No she doesn't, I managed not to say. *Gambit* is an opening manoeuvre or proposition, from a term used in chess for an opening move. My friend's daughter liked the whole *gamut* – the entire range.

Beware of Greeks . . .

Here's another phenomenon that can get you into trouble: Hellenomania. It means a madness for things Greek and is sometimes casually extended to embrace Latin words, too: the point is that it involves a long word of classical origin when a shorter and/or more familiar one will do perfectly well. It's using *felicitous* when you mean *apt*, *pellucid* when you mean *clear* and *subfusc* when you mean *gloomy*. Of course there are times when the grander words are appropriate – we're all entitled to our poetic or our erudite moments – but if you overdo it you risk being accused of pretentiousness (or attitudinizing or rodomontade). Or you may simply find people staring at you because they don't know what you're talking about.

Include me in (or out)

Reading an article about the pros and cons of the United Kingdom leaving the European Union, I learned that six prominent retired politicians – *including A, B, C, D, E and F* – were in favour of our staying in. Skimming lightly over the politics and the economics, let's look at the word *including*. *To include* means (among other things) 'to contain as a constituent part of a whole'. It doesn't mean 'to make up the whole', which would be *to comprise* or *to consist of*.

Thus, Philip Pullman's *His Dark Materials* trilogy *includes Northern Lights* (or *The Golden Compass* if you prefer), but it *comprises* or *consists of Northern Lights*, *The Subtle Knife* and *The Amber Spyglass*. The instruments in a classic string quartet *include* two violins, but *comprise* two violins, a viola and a cello.

In the retired politicians example, the *including* simply isn't necessary: *six retired politicians* – A, B, C, D, E and F [all six of them] – would have been correct, as would *six former retired politicians, including A and B*. A similar construction might refer to *Enid Blyton's Famous Five* – *Anne, Dick, George, Julian and Timmy* – or to *Enid Blyton's Famous Five, including the dog Timmy. Including*, in other words, refers to part of the whole, not to the whole itself.

As for *comprising* and *consisting of*, a single entity *consists of* or *comprises* or *is composed of* various ingredients; the ingredients *comprise* the whole.

You'll notice that *comprised of* doesn't crop up in this list of options: it's wrong. But there is always a get-out clause: if in doubt, use *make up* or *is made up* of instead:

Two violins, a viola and a cello make up a classic string quartet.

A classic string quartet is made up of two violins, a viola and a cello.

CHAPTER 5

Like a coiled spring

Tautologies and sillinesses

In the 2016 film of *Dad's Army*, Sergeant Wilson describes the men of his platoon as being ready to pounce 'like a coiled spring'.

'Every spring is coiled, Wilson,' says Captain Mainwaring tartly.

Fans of *Dad's Army* will know (and I'm going to ask those who are unfamiliar with this very Bristish comedy to take my word for it) that Captain Mainwaring isn't right very often, but he has a point here. Every spring is indeed coiled, just as every haven is safe, every gift free and every scrutiny close. Yet modern English is riddled with expressions like these – known as tautologies, redundancies or pleonasms – and many of them are so common that they have become clichés.

Your salary may be *adequate*, for example, or it may be *enough* for your needs, but *adequate enough* is too much of a good thing. As is the near-ubiquitous *the reason is because.* Either *the reason is (that)* or *it has happened because* – not both.

The same applies to *I've tried to do this as accurately as possible.* Go for either *I've tried to do this accurately* or *I've done this as accurately as possible.*

Moreover, winning a prize *three consecutive years in a row* may be praiseworthy, but it isn't good English. *Consecutive years* are by definition *in a row.*

In the same spirit, I laughed when I read – in a book published by a respectable university press – about someone being *originally born in New York.* Taken at face value, it suggests that he might have had a spiritual rebirth once he moved to the West Coast, which I'm reasonably certain is not what was meant. Delete that *originally.*

My local theatre warned that there would be smoking (on the stage) *throughout the duration of* the performance of a certain play. I saw that production and can vouch for the fact that there was smoking *throughout* the performance, or *for the duration of* the performance but, again, not both.

You'd think that theatres, for whom words are the life blood, would be more careful. But no: they have also been known to ask you to *pre-order your interval drinks in advance.* And, although it isn't a tautology as such, it's common knowledge in the theatre that the first half is generally longer than the second (for the comfort of those who have been drinking during the interval and don't want to wait too long for a bathroom break). I have no problem with the principle – I've been known to drink during intervals myself – but convert 'half' to '50 per cent' and you'll see that it's not quite right.

A more intellectual version of the same mistake: a distinguished actor said, in a television documentary about *The Merchant of Venice*, that there were 'two main halves of the play – the Portia half and the Shylock half'. You know exactly what he means, but ... And in similar vein, the compere of a variety show that was long enough to justify two intervals used to announce, late in the evening and with great gusto, that the curtain was about to go up on the *third half.* He meant it as a joke, but no one in the audience ever seemed to notice. Perhaps they'd pre-ordered too many drinks in advance.

Moving from theatre to cinema, we find a newspaper article about the *Star Wars* franchise referring to *Return of the Jedi* as 'the third sequel'. Is this poor fact-checking or poor use of language? A sequel is something that follows something else, so *Return of the Jedi*, as even non-nerds will know, is the third part of the trilogy or the third film in the original series, but it is only the second sequel.

Anti-tautology crusaders seem to have lost the battle against *PIN number*, but I stick to my guns: what do the people who say it think the N stands for? There's also the concept in the UK education world of a NQT – a Newly Qualified Teacher, one who has

Irregardless

A tautology contained within a single word! This has arisen through a confusion between *regardless* and *irrespective*, both of which are actually words. The OED acknowledges the existence of *irregardless* 'in nonstandard or humorous use', which means that it is sneaking round the barricades and making its way into the language. For the moment, though, it's best avoided.

passed the exams but not yet completed the induction programme. Perhaps inevitably, this leads to people referring to NQT teachers. In due course, successful NQTs attain what is widely described as QTS status, with no prizes for guessing what the S stands for.

If in doubt about expressions that trip readily off the tongue, consider what their opposites might mean. If they are silly or a contradiction in terms, what you are saying is probably silly too. *Dangerous haven*? I rest my case.

- My local paper recently wrote about the *future direction* an up-and-coming area was taking as development continued. Could it have had a *past direction*? No. Dispense with 'future' and you have something that makes sense.

- An *unsubstantiated* or *unconfirmed rumour* is another case in point. The moment you can substantiate or confirm it, it ceases to be a rumour and becomes a report, an account or a piece of news. *Unconfirmed report*, therefore, is fine, because the word *report* is neutral – it doesn't convey either belief or disbelief.

- The *protagonist* of a play or story is the principal character. You can't have a *minor protagonist*, so you don't have a *main protagonist* either.

- There's no need to say that, in a difficult situation, someone *can face potential problems.* The uncertainty of *can* is repeated in *potential*, so either *faces potential problems* or *can face problems* is warning enough.

- Be wary of a book whose publicity describes it as a *helpful guide*. How much use would an *unhelpful guide* be?

- A gift box of toiletries that I was given for Christmas included something whose packaging described it as *cleansing soap*, as if there were any other kind. It also, bizarrely, boasted that it was a limited edition, suggesting that instead of washing with it I might hold on to it for a while and sell it at a profit. (I didn't, so I'll never know what it would have been worth in five years' time.)

- You don't *share together*: the whole point of sharing is that you do it together. So you may *share a bed* or *go to bed together*; you may *share a dessert* or *order one dessert and two spoons*. The caption to a photograph of Claire Foy, playing Queen Elizabeth II in the TV series *The Crown* and published alongside one of Her Majesty taken some decades ago, said that she 'shared a striking resemblance with the young Queen Elizabeth'. Certainly in the photos they looked quite alike, so the actor *has* or *bears* a resemblance to the monarch. But if the Queen and Claire Foy *share* a resemblance it must be a resemblance *to* something else. Perhaps they both look like the young Helen Mirren.

- And when did we start saying *work colleagues*? A colleague is by definition someone with whom one works. (Do you have *play colleagues*? I don't. Or none that it seems appropriate to mention here.) Add something more specific, by all means: you can have *teaching colleagues* or *nursing colleagues* or *army colleagues*, but *work colleagues* is a waste of a word.

- In a documentary that ought to have known better, I heard *summarizing in a nutshell*, *reverting back* and *a tendency to over-exaggerate*. Within the space of two hours. Hmm.

Added bonus? *Final conclusion*? *Sum total*? *Honest truth*? They all become nonsenses if you submit them to *close scrutiny*.

What's odd is . . .

If you type the same word twice in a Word document, that irritating red squiggle will appear to point out your error. But there are occasions when *is is* (or *was was* or the like) is correct, though you may like to add a comma or take a small pause for breath:

> *That isn't a mishap. What it is* [comma/pause for breath] *is a complete disaster.*
> *He wasn't a criminal exactly. What he was, was a forty-year-old juvenile delinquent.*

I suspect it is because of this that people have taken to saying, 'the thing is is'. There's no justification for this, however. Sentences such as:

> *The thing is, he doesn't know what he's doing* or
> *The point is, you need to make him understand*

are perfectly correct; they aren't tongue twisters and they don't (to my ear, at least) sound awkward or in any other sense wrong. But 'the thing is is' is becoming increasingly common and (IMHO) should be stamped on while we still have the chance.

Never heard anyone saying it? Start listening, now that I've mentioned it. You will.

Transport for London – the company that runs, as its name suggests, public transport in the UK capital – has developed an annoying tendency of announcing that, on the Underground, for example, 'the District Line is partially closed between Turnham Green and Richmond'. Annoying not only because it makes it more difficult to get to Chiswick for tea, but because that statement simply isn't true. The District Line is partially closed, certainly, but it is *completely* closed between the two stations specified. If it was genuinely *partially closed* between Turnham Green and Richmond, it might mean that the track was closed between two of the four stops in question but open the rest of the way – in which case, why not say so?

I haven't heard anyone but Transport for London using this turn of phrase. Overground train companies refer to 'planned engineering works' and offer a *rail replacement bus service* – yet another accumulation of nouns of the kind referred to on page 168. Where did this expression come from? Even if you are prepared to tolerate the nounspeak, it should surely be either a *train replacement bus service* or a *rail replacement road service*.

TfL has a number of its own ways of speaking. I recently heard a pre-recorded voice alerting me to delays on the Northern Line and asking me to listen for further messages. A strangely intimate word, I thought: a message is the private thing you leave on someone's voicemail or put optimistically into a bottle if you are shipwrecked on a desert island; when you want to tell hundreds of thousands of passengers that their tickets will be valid on local buses, this is surely an *announcement*.

This is how rumours start

A biographical note on a distinguished author told me that she was *a former graduate of the University of East Anglia.* What had she done, I wondered. Presumably something scandalous in order to be stripped of her degree. I think we should be told.

And I know it has been said before, and we have to blame our Health-and-Safety-obsessed culture, but does a packet of sleeping pills really need to carry the warning that it may cause drowsiness?

Enough. If I go on, I'll find myself talking about the *end result* of a *personal friend* finding herself in *close proximity* with a *dangerous menace*, which turned out to be an *unexpected surprise* and a *sad misfortune*.

CHAPTER 6

A certain I don't know what

Foreign words and expressions

There are two tiny abbreviations, deeply entrenched in our everyday usage and meaning completely different things, that are easy to confuse if you don't happen to know Latin: *i.e.* and *e.g.*

I.e. is short for *id est*, which means 'that is'; *e.g.* means *exempli gratia* – 'for example'. One way of remembering which is which is to say that *i.e.* is 'in effect' and *e.g.* 'example given'. It's not an accurate translation, but it's not meant to be: it's a memory aid. If it helps, use it.

Alternatively, you could think of *i.e.* as meaning 'includes everything': you use it when you mean 'in other words, namely', when what follows is the same as what went before, with nothing left out. If you mean 'for example, such as, including', so that the following list contains examples of what you are talking about but there *is* something left out, you need *e.g.*

For example. A guide to help librarians assess how their online resources were being used referred to *the total resource usage (e.g. number of downloads)*. A librarian who was new to the system but who knew what *e.g.* meant would assume that counting the number of downloads was one possible way of establishing total usage, but that there were others he didn't know about. In fact, the writer means *i.e.* – total resource usage is *the same thing* as the number of downloads. Counting downloads isn't *one* of the ways of establishing total usage; it is the *only* way.

Et cetera, et cetera, et cetera

If you find the above complicated, dispense with the Latin altogether: write *for example* or *that is* in full. Only on character-restricted Twitter will this make a difference.

George Orwell would probably have approved: he advised writers never to use a foreign phrase if they could think of an everyday English equivalent. That said, dispensing with Latin altogether isn't easy. Here's a selection of Latin expressions, some of them so familiar that we may not even realize they are foreign.

ad hoc (literally 'towards this'). Used to mean 'for the moment, temporary' as in *an* ad hoc *arrangement that will have to do until we can sort out something permanent.*

ad lib (short for **ad libitum**, 'according to pleasure'). What you do when you haven't prepared a speech or you're a stand-up comedian being heckled. *I'd left ten minutes for questions and no one asked any, so I had to* ad lib *for the rest of the time.*

ad nauseam ('to sickness'). To the point of making someone feel sick – usually metaphorically. *He went on and on* ad nauseam *about the same old things. Ad infinitum* ('to infinity') is used in much the same way, without the concern about having to clear up the mess afterwards.

bona fide ('with good faith'). Genuine. *You can't come in unless you can prove that you are a* bona fide *member of the club.*

de facto ('from the fact'). Not legally recognized but doing the job anyway. *When her father grew too old to cope, she became* de facto *manager of the estate.* The opposite, used in law but not much in common parlance, is *de iure*, 'by law'.

et al (short for **et alia**, 'and other things'). Often used to mean 'and other people', and rather disparaging. *The usual gang was there: Annabel, Jocelyn, Zoe* et al.

et cetera ('and the rest'). Often written as etc. and used to mean 'and so on, and more of the same'. *He's become obsessed with fancy vegetables – pink and white beetroot, Russian kale,* etc.' Repeating the phrase – *et cetera, et cetera* or even *et cetera, et cetera, et cetera* – suggests that you are getting fed up with the subject, whatever it may be.

NB (short for **nota bene**, 'note well'). Used to draw particular attention to an important point. NB *I am not in the office next week, so someone else will have to deal with this.*

per cent (short for **per centum**, 'for each hundred'). A way of expressing a fraction: 10 per cent means ten out of every hundred, or one tenth.

per se ('in itself'). Intrinsically, essentially. *He didn't object to stockbrokers* per se, *he just wasn't sure he wanted his daughter to marry one.*

PS (short for **post scriptum**, 'after writing'). An abbreviation used after the signature in a letter, to indicate an addition.

quid pro quo ('what for what'). A reciprocal arrangement. *He helps me with my tax return, so I give him free piano lessons as a* quid pro quo.

sic ('thus'). Written, usually in square brackets, after something that looks wrong, to show that the mistake is intentional or that it appeared in an original that is being quoted: *The greengrocer was offering banana's and potato's* [sic].

status quo ('condition in which'). Used to mean 'the current position, the condition in which things are now': *The* status quo *is completely unacceptable; we need to make radical changes.*

vice versa ('the other way around'). *We could eat in tonight and go out for dinner tomorrow, or* vice versa – whichever you prefer.

Plus ça change

In some of the above examples you could avoid the Latin: 'She effectively managed the estate' would serve the purpose just as well as 'She became de facto manager.' But Latin is not the only foreign language from which English has borrowed words and phrases we use every day. Where would we be without *faux pas* and *joie de vivre*; *femmes fatales* and *idées fixes*;

paparazzi, aficionados and *angst*? Clear-sighted man that he was, Orwell recognized the problem: his final piece of advice was 'Break any of these rules sooner than say anything outright barbarous.'

So, on the basis that I can argue that I have Orwell's blessing, here are some more foreign expressions, in addition to those just mentioned and French unless otherwise stated, without which I feel English would lack that certain I don't know what.

carte blanche – you could give someone a *white card* or a *blank card*, but they'd have to ask you what you meant them to do with it. With a *carte blanche*, they can do what they like.

chutzpah – yes, we have lots of words that mean *cheek*, *brass neck*, *impudence*, *nerve*, but nothing conveys shameless audacity quite as effectively as this Yiddish word.

coup d'état – if ever I decide to overthrow the government, I'm not going to call it a *blow of state*. No one would take me seriously. Come to think of it, if I take to directing plays, I don't want to pull off a *blow of theatre*, either.

déjà vu – seen it all before? Maybe, but a sense of *déjà vu* can send shivers down your spine in a way that its English equivalent can't.

doppelgänger – unless you are a Freudian or a devotee of alternative-reality games, you may have only a vague idea of what this German term means, but even so you'll surely admit that *double goer* doesn't sound nearly as good.

entrepreneur – there is a little-used English equivalent to this word – *enterpriser*, which I came across recently as the answer to a crossword clue but have never seen anywhere else. We've been preferring the French version for the better part of two centuries.

fait accompli – true, *done deed* means much the same thing, but surely lacks the *flair*, the *élan* or the *panache* of the French.

incognito is simply an Italian word for *unknown* or *disguised*, but it carries a bit more *brio*. Anybody can put on dark glasses and claim to be in disguise; only a spy or a celebrity can really be *incognito*.

kitsch – like *nouveau riche* (see page 152), this is a word that communicates a wealth of scorn. You can say *tat* in a supercilious way – to indicate that you wouldn't be seen dead with something as tasteless as that in *your* home – but there's something about the way you can spit the German word that conveys even more contempt.

machismo – *male chauvinism* is slightly different: you can be a chauvinist without being *macho*. *Macho* is the ordinary Spanish word for *male*, but it also implies the aggressive pride in being male, the physical vigour and the tendency to drink and womanize that we suggest when we use it in English. There is no better established word in English that can convey so much in so few syllables.

masseur – do you really want to take most of your clothes off and be pummelled by a *massager*?

mot juste – P. G. Wodehouse, in *Ring for Jeeves*, describes a romantically inclined woman sitting in a moonlit garden thinking about her beloved and observes that 'a stylist like the late Gustave Flaubert, tireless in his quest of the *mot juste*, would have had no hesitation in describing her mood as mushy'. Translate *mot juste* into 'right word' and it isn't anything like as funny.

nouveau riche/parvenu – what I like about these terms is that they are so dismissive. *Upstart* – a reasonable alternative to *parvenu* – is pretty dismissive too, but nothing in English better conveys the upper-class contempt for the newly minted, tasteless jewellery, the flashy cars and the ostentatious generosity that are encapsulated in *nouveau riche*.

sangfroid – not at all the same as *cold-bloodedness*, although 'cold blood' is the literal translation. *Sangfroid* is more like the traditional British stiff upper lip, but perhaps rather more *debonair*.

schadenfreude – a German word that crops up again and again in surveys of English-speakers' favourites: the pleasure we feel at someone else's misfortune. The American writer Gore Vidal came closest to an equivalent when he said, 'Every time a friend succeeds, something inside me dies.' It is perhaps not very gracious of us to have adopted this word so enthusiastically while ignoring its near-opposite *gönnen*, 'not to begrudge someone something, to be gladdened by their good fortune'.

schlep – another fine Yiddish word. For some reason, 'Isn't that a bit of a *schlep* for you?' sounds more sympathetic than 'Do you want to go that far?' and makes it easier for the other person to say, 'Let's meet half way.'

tête à tête – a *head-to-head* may be all very well for a televised political debate or for betting on a sporting fixture, but an intimate encounter requires the French.

vendetta – with its connection to Mafia-ridden southern Italy, this is just that little bit fiercer and more long-lasting than a feud. And speaking of the Mafia, you wouldn't feel terribly intimidated by an organization called Our Thing, would you?

A word of caution: if you want to use these expressions, make sure you use them correctly. Not so long ago I did a series of radio interviews on a point of grammar that had been in the news. A number of my interviewers broadened the subject to include other aspects of language and more than one mentioned their particular *faux pas*. I assumed (silently, I'm happy to say) they meant that they made a recurrent mistake, that there was a certain issue of grammar or usage they found it difficult to grasp. No. It transpired they were all – and I think this happened three times in the space of one morning – talking about mistakes other people made that really annoyed them. Not a *faux pas* (a false step) at all, in fact, but a *bête noire*, a 'black beast' or pet hate.

Et pourquoi pas?

One of the reasons English is such a rich and varied language is that we have always drawn on a wide range of sources, as the previous section shows. Celtic, Anglo-Saxon, Norse, Latin, Norman French – they have all been in the mix for almost a thousand years. Later, it helped that we Brits had an empire from whose outposts we could draw *bamboo*, *calico*, *compound*, *gong*, *jumbo*, *jungle*, *kangaroo*, *safari*, *shampoo*, *typhoon* and *voodoo*.

So if over the years we have chosen to borrow these

words and expressions, what's to stop us carrying on doing it? Here are some words, culled from various 'other languages have these words, so why don't we?' websites, that it is very tempting to adopt or translate.

akihi (Hawaiian) – forgetting directions immediately after you hear them.

Drachenfutter (German) – the kind of 'please forgive me' present that husbands give their wives after staying out late and coming home drunk. It's no small part of this word's charm that it translates as 'dragon fodder'.

halatnost (Russian) – 'dressing-gownness', that feeling of apathy that makes it too much of an effort to get dressed and get on with your day.

hanyauku (RuKwangali) – walking on tiptoes across hot sand. RuKwangali is one of the national languages of Namibia, home of the world's most magnificent sand dunes. It may be true to say that the Namibians need this word more than we do, but I'm sure they can afford to share it.

hyppytyynytyydytys (Finnish) – the satisfaction of sitting (or bouncing) on a bouncy cushion. Finnish also boasts the word *juoksentelisinkohan*, which means 'I wonder if I should perhaps just run around aimlessly'. Yes, it's a long word, but it has a lot of value packed into it. You can see why the Finns have a reputation for being taciturn: it is said that, having spent a lot of their history being ruled either by Sweden or by Russia and having won their independence only a century ago, they have too much national pride to speak any language but their own – and that is just too difficult, so they keep quiet.

I digress.

iktsuarpok (Inuit) – going outside to check if anyone is coming. A word that clearly needs updating to include constantly checking your phone to see if a special person has rung.

Neidbau (German) – something constructed just to annoy the neighbour. The website on which I found this word illustrated it with a topiary of someone flashing their naked buttocks towards the garden fence.

Schnappsidee (German) – a crazy, drink-induced idea. We've all had them. Maybe we could translate this and call it a *booze wave*.

tingo (Pascuense) – the act of 'borrowing' objects you like from the house of a friend one by one over a period of time, until you have eventually acquired all of them. It says something about the culture of Easter Island that they need a word for this, but I have noticed that the Western world is full of people who don't return books . . .

Torschlusspanik (German) – literally 'gate-closing panic', idiomatically 'the fear of opportunities diminishing as one grows older'.

tsundoku (Japanese) – literally 'reading pile', the result of buying books and not reading them. With, presumably, associated guilt. I wonder if there should be a special subsection to apply to, say, *Clarissa*, *A Brief History of Time* and some of the longer Man Booker winners.

utepils (Norwegian) – a beer drunk outside on a sunny day, especially the first of the season when the long winter is finally showing signs of subsiding.

Closer to home, the Scots are a rich source of words that deserve to be more widely used. There's *fankle*, meaning a tangle, particularly of all those wires behind the television set. There's *grue*, shivering or shuddering, from which we derive *gruesome*; *jirbling*, spilling liquid by pouring with an unsteady hand; and *tartling*, hesitating when you recognize someone but can't remember their name. Shouldn't the English entice these south of the border?

There ought to be a word for it

Even without drawing on existing foreign words, we find gaps in our language. If when you come back from holiday you have to deal with a *backlog*, should the panic you go into before going away have to do with a *forelog* or *frontlog*? And what happens before an *aftermath*?

CHAPTER 7

Eligibility and scheme benefit criteria apply

The modern passion for jargon and gobbledygook

Although the earliest meaning of the word *jargon* refers to birdsong, twittering or chattering, most of us would think of it as a contemptuous term, applied, as the OED puts it, 'to any mode of speech abounding in unfamiliar terms, or peculiar to a particular set of persons'. By way of illustration, the OED's citations include references to *the jargon of the law*, *much metaphysical jargon* and *the jargon of the German mystic.*

Jargon has its uses: to insiders, it is a form of shorthand. One grammarian may talk to another about phrasal verbs or formal and notional agreement, secure in the knowledge that they will both understand. An outsider will say, 'Sorry? What?' and have to be told that a phrasal verb is something like *to turn up* [in time for the debate] or *to look after* [a dog while its owner is on holiday], and that formal and notional agreement are ways of dealing with the question of whether *the team is* or *are* likely to go through to the final. 'Oh, okay,' says the outsider, while the grammarian taps her fingers in impatience because she *knows* all this. An astrologer can tell a well-informed client that Jupiter aligns with Mars without having to go into the detail of what (if anything) this means. When everyone is in the know, jargon saves time.

But somewhere along the line jargon-as-shorthand crossed an invisible line and became jargon-as-nonsense. It's not that people deliberately set out to mislead; it's that they seem to think that saying something straightforward, that everyone can understand, is wrong. It's simple, so it must be unprofessional. The most shameful example of this I have come across lately was from a publisher of children's books (that's why I say it is shameful – of all professions in the land, you'd think this would be the one that laid most emphasis on clear communication). Referring to the new cover design of a children's classic, she was quoted as saying, 'The cover is still rooted in the editorial vision.' Does this mean *anything* other than 'the cover gives some idea of what the book is about' or 'the illustration is vaguely related to the book's content'?

A senior figure in the publishing world was quoted as saying, with reference to the pricing of ebooks, that his company faced the challenge of maintaining 'the value perception of our quality content'. I assume this means encouraging people to pay good money for good books, but it can hardly be described as crystal clear.

Yet another publisher, writing about a proposed change of warehousing arrangements, reassured customers that 'our *migration plan* has been designed to ensure service is maintained throughout'. I'm sorry, but what would have been wrong with *move* in that sentence? And, as an aside, does a move from Essex to Lincolnshire (a distance of about 200 km) count as a migration? I'm guessing a sooty shearwater or a humpback whale might have something to say about that.

At the time of writing, it is being predicted that the traditionally shabby eastern part of Oxford Street in London is about to become fashionable. Various retailers are opening 'statement' stores there. I frankly have no idea what this means. What statement are they making? Perhaps their goods will be *fashion forward*, as the catalogue of an exhibition of fashion recently put it: surely *at the forefront of fashion* or *pushing the boundaries of fashion* would have been clearer.

The boom period for jargon-for-the-sake-of-it seems to have been the 1980s: that era of entrepreneurship when bright young men in red braces were working sixteen-hour days, making obscene sums of money and using expressions such as *blue-sky thinking, a wake-up call* and *worst-case scenario*. While these were all once original and expressive turns of phrase – created by people who were capable of *thinking outside the box* – they evolved from ingenious to commonplace to cliché in a remarkably short time. Wanting a candidate for a job to *hit the ground running* or keeping a colleague *in the loop* by giving them the *heads-up* on a recent development has become the stuff of satire, a way for a writer to convey a character's insincerity and determination to toe the company line. Such a person would say, 'We'll be looking to plug into your skill set going forward' rather than 'In the future we'll want to make use of your various skills.' She would never refer to *clients*: it would always be *our client base*.

In that last paragraph, by the way, *toe* is right. The idiom comes from the idea of putting your toe against (but not over) the starting line at the beginning of a race. It has nothing to do with *towing* a caravan or a broken-down car.

Going back to candidates for jobs, when did we start saying 'role' instead of 'job'? And why? What's so demeaning about working for a living? Or is it that we are all just acting a part when we go to the office?

A journalistic favourite of recent years is *looks set to*, as in 'the drop-in centre *looks set to close* when funding is withdrawn next year'. This one baffles me. There is, after all, something inherently firm about the word set. A jelly is ready to eat when it is set (okay, it wobbles a bit, but that's the nature of jelly). To an athlete, *set* is the instruction immediately before *go*: you'd better be ready or you'll be left behind. If you set a good example, you're doing something in a clear, unequivocal way. But that poor drop-in centre is only *likely* to close. Or, if the decision is final, *it is to close or it is going to close* – there's no *looking* about it.

Then there is local government. One local authority in southern England appointed a working party to make a Strategic Environmental Assessment (SEA) of an area that had been proposed for development. As part of the background to its report, the working party advised:

The methodology for the assessment is intended to be proportionate to the task of assessing the modest development proposals of a Neighbourhood Plan in a relatively small parish area. It focuses only on the requirements of SEA and does not extend to cover the wider sustainability attributes of a Sustainability Appraisal.

In other words, the assessment does what it sets out to do and nothing else. Perfectly reasonable, but why couldn't they say so? Or, indeed, why didn't it go without saying?

Politicians are just as bad: the following paragraph comes from a report on a speech by a former Prime Minister of New Zealand, Helen Clark, entitled 'A Young

Take a memo

The play *The Memorandum* by Czech author-turned-president Václav Havel revolves around a new language called Ptydepe (a word made up by the author), which is designed to avoid the unreliability and ambiguity of 'natural' languages. The central character receives a memo informing him of his bosses' views on the new language. Unfortunately he can't read it – because it is written in Ptydepe. A secretary in the office can read the language, but doesn't have a permit to translate it. She can't get the permit because the person authorized to give out permits can't issue them for documents she doesn't understand, and she won't understand them until they have been translated. Small wonder that Ptydepe – a language that has six words for *boo* and whose longest word, at 319 letters, means a *wombat* – has passed into Czech as meaning something along the lines of gobbledygook. It should be a lesson to us all.

Commonwealth: Youth, Innovation and Sustainable Development':

'How could the current global offer [to youth] be improved?' the speaker wanted to know. Here before us, evidently, was 'an opportunity to reset the compass' by forming 'an all-of-society agenda', harnessing new

digital technologies and social media that permit 'tremendous outreach to the global public' and 'global citizenry'.

The journalist who wrote this went on to refer to George Orwell's *Nineteen Eighty-Four,* in which the novelist drew attention to

a trait which his fictional totalitarian state encouraged in its citizens, a habit that passed for communication but which was actually something else. He called it duckspeak: speech in which the mind was bypassed and sentences proceeded directly from the larynx. This habit was of course fatal to clear thinking.

If we fall into the habit of resetting compasses and forming all-of-society agendas, we'll be waddling along in duckspeak before we know where we are.

I mentioned George Orwell's guidelines for writers earlier; one of them was 'Never use a metaphor, simile or other figure of speech which you are used to seeing in print'. On that basis, here is a short list of expressions, in addition to those already mentioned, that I would ban if I were Big Brother:

- *bottom line* (unless you are talking about a set of accounts)

- *cutting edge* (unless you are talking about knives)

- *the elephant in the room* (unless there is one)

- *fire-fighting* (unless a genuine conflagration is involved)

- *firing on all cylinders* (unless you are talking about a car)

- *a learning curve*

- *a level playing field*

- *moving the goalposts* (unless you are changing a soccer field into a rugby field)

- *on message*

- *a paradigm shift*

- *reinventing the wheel*

- *running it up the flagpole to see who salutes it*

- *a safe pair of hands*

- *seeing how it will pan out*

- *singing from the same song sheet* (unless you are in a choir) and *on the same page* (unless you are in a reading group)

- *taking your eye off the ball*

- *touching base* (unless you are playing baseball)

- *win-win situation* (for some reason *lose-lose* or *win-*

lose are more acceptable: they seem to be used more rarely and more thoughtfully, perhaps because the people who rely on expressions such as these are incurable optimists)

- *window of opportunity*

At the end of the day is in a subsection of this list, because while it is a ludicrous thing to say at ten o'clock in the morning (and should therefore be banned), I bracket it with *in fairness, to be fair, to be honest* and *to tell the truth* as meaningless sentence fillers: is our being fair, honest and truthful so rare that we have to draw attention to it?

I don't suggest for one moment that my list is comprehensive. This is a real growth area for those who want to moan about the way English is going.

Needles and pins

Not so much jargon as an odd euphemism. I was giving blood and the beeper went off to indicate that the required 470 ml had left my veins. A nurse came along and said, 'I'll just take your donation down for you.' She was very sweet and I appreciate that she was trying to make me feel comfortable, but 'I'll just take the needle out of your arm' wouldn't have been offensive. It's not as if I didn't realize there was a needle in my arm.

Finally, something I seem to be hearing increasingly often: politicians who are becoming more outspoken on a given subject are described as *ramping up* their rhetoric. Intriguingly, *ramp* as a verb was first used in the 1980s in the context of driving up the prices of shares in order to make a quick and not necessarily legal profit. Just saying.

Noun accumulation fatuity fiasco

Headline writers, whether they are working in newspapers, in advertising or on websites, need to fit their copy into the available space. Their skill lies in being both comprehensible and eye-catching in a very few words, and they can't afford to waste valuable inches with boring little fillers such as *of the*. This leads to the phenomenon known as *nounspeak*: agglomerating nouns (or lumping them together, if you prefer) to form clunky, repetitive and impersonal phrases.

Bruce D. Price, the American journalist who coined the term, points out that English has traditionally accepted two-noun terms (the examples he gives include *book store*, *love affair* and *state university*). But in the last half-century or so we have developed a tolerance of, even an admiration for, longer and longer noun-heavy expressions, such as *space ship booster rocket ignition system.* Price's objections are to repetition (*subject matter* and *transition period* instead of *subject* and *transition*), depersonalization (*consumer discontent* – a more abstract concept than the real people who are *discontented consumers*) and the general weakening of expressions through the lack of punchy verbs (*accomplishing pest control* rather than *controlling pests*).

Business people are often guilty of using a lot of this terminology: I recently came across a company whose aim was to *gain skills in customer acquisition*. As a way of *growing the business*, perhaps? But they aren't the only ones: politicians love it, too. Back in the 1960s, US President Lyndon Johnson objected to the codename Masher, used for an operation during the Vietnam War, because it didn't have the right *pacification emphasis.* And in his 2004 State of the Union address, at the height of the controversy over the Second Iraq War, President George W. Bush referred to *dozens of weapons of mass destruction-related program activities.* The world of IT is another guilty party, with expressions such as *user activity data* and *potential total usage outputs* abounding.

To go back to the headline writers, I have another objection to all this: lack of sense. *Nature* magazine contained an article about a university seeking private donations *to offset climate funding crunch*. How can you fund climate? What would have been wrong with *to fund climate-change research*, which is presumably what it means? It has the advantage of being one character shorter, and it makes sense. And this sort of nonsense isn't confined to headlines: if I want to benefit from a certain store's new loyalty card, the small print warns me that *eligibility and scheme benefit qualification criteria apply*. I assume that means I must be over eighteen and not saddled with debt, but there must surely have been a less brain-numbing way of expressing it. The online *Journal of Finance* offers *Information in the Term Structure of Yield Curve Volatility.* I can't suggest an alternative there, as I have absolutely no idea what it means.

Then there is an issue of crassness, another regular feature of nounspeak headlines. While the meaning is clear enough, *tunnel death cash* is surely an insensitive way to describe the compensation paid to a widow whose husband had died in an accident during the building of an underground railway – particularly as it is highly unlikely that the payment was to be made in cash.

Human resources is another prime example: a resource is something you can draw on and – as we are only too aware when it comes to *natural resources* – exhaust. There's something inherently dehumanizing about considering your employees, or indeed any member of the human race, as a resource.

Any noun can be verbed

Users of British English who object to Americanisms are particularly vociferous about this issue. In computer-speak the verb *to access* (as in *to access a site* or *to access a piece of information*) has wide currency, but I would still wince – and not for moral reasons – at the idea of a burglar *accessing* (rather than *gaining access to*) a building. But we have to be careful what we dismiss as an encroaching Americanism: *alphabetize*, which offends those who can't see anything wrong with *putting things into alphabetical order*, goes back to the seventeenth century and has been used on this side of the Atlantic every bit as much as the other. *Propagandize*, a back-formation from *propaganda*, sounded like an Orwellian piece of Newspeak when used by former US Secretary of Defense Donald Rumsfeld, but in fact has a history stretching back 150 years.

However, here are a few that I think we should strive to avoid. I have a personal aversion for *to author*, when what is meant is *to write*. *To pen* is just as bad, particularly given the unlikelihood of a pen being involved. And *to scribe* is surely just pretentious. The common feature of most of the following is that they go for brevity, packing into one word what traditional British English expresses in three or four. I'm all in favour of avoiding long-windedness, but there is surely some sort of middle ground to be found here.

To critique: go for *to criticize*, if that is what you mean; in academic circles you would *write a critique of*, say, a paper that had been put out for peer review.

To exit (a vehicle): Yes, English teachers always told you not to use *get*, but here's one instance where I think it's the natural choice – an actor *exits* the stage, but you and I *get off* the bus or the train.

To grow (a business): you *grow* plants, or your hair if you want to change its style; you *expand* a business.

To helm when what you mean is *to lead*, as in *to helm the project going forward.* A draft addition to the OED dated 2007 gives what was originally a US definition of *to helm* as *to direct* (*a film, television programme*, etc.) and has a citation from as long ago as 1930. But the OED is recording usage, not prescribing correct or elegant prose. In other words, we don't have to like it or use it just because it is in the dictionary.

To impact (the situation in the Middle East, perhaps) – if you insist on brevity, *effect* is a good alternative; otherwise *have an impact* (or *an effect*) *on*.

To partner with (another organization). You *partner* someone at bridge or on the dance floor; in business you *go into partnership*.

To pressure someone into doing something is surely no improvement on *to pressurize* or *to put pressure on*.

To sideline is simply ugly shorthand for *to put on the sidelines*.

But not all verbing is bad. It's hard to object to a street artist describing a wall he had *graffitied* – unless, I suppose, you have a rooted objection to street art – nor to Dylan Thomas's elderly sea captain dreaming of 'the one love of his sea-life that was *sardined* with women'. When the *Times* journalist Matthew Parris wrote about the dangers of lumping people of different races together under the heading 'Black and Minority Ethnic', his warning that '*topiarising* data into unnatural shapes only distorts and offends' created an evocative new verb from a well-established noun.

On a more trivial level, at dinner at a friend's house recently the host told us she was *guinea-pigging* us – trying out a recipe that she hadn't made before. Lovely word, delicious pudding; we revelled in both.

Some adjectives can be verbed, too, as when a certain multinational energy company was described as having *grubbied its reputation*. I rather like this, which just shows what a personal matter the whole business is.

Unnecessary prepositions

We seem to be introducing more and more of these. Here are a few of my personal 'must to avoids'.

Head up, as in *to head up an enquiry*. What's wrong with *heading an inquiry*? And, to revert to the point about 'if the opposite is silly, the chances are this is silly too' (see page 139), who ever heard of *heading down an inquiry*?

Next up: that favourite of television announcers who are merely telling us what is on *next*.

Ahead of refers to position, not time, as in *he went ahead of the rest of the party to check that the path was safe*. But increasingly we hear sentences such as *the President is holding a meeting with advisors ahead of the international summit.* Why not *in preparation for*, *prior to* or simply *before*?

A report on the bestselling books of 2015 told us that *Elena Ferrante's* My Brilliant Friend *... was the highest-earning translated title of the year ... narrowly beating out Lars Myttling's* Norwegian Wood. What on earth is that *out* doing there? You can *beat out* a rhythm on a drum or *beat out* a tattoo if you knock loudly on a door, but *beating out* a rival is surely uncalled for.

Two Americanisms I'd prefer to resist: *too large of* as in *too large of a scope for the project*. Let's just leave out the *of* and see if anyone complains. And *the lack of having a ...* The example that caught my eye was *the lack of having a clear reporting structure*. I'd have thought that *the lack of a clear reporting structure* made life complicated enough.

. . . and a couple of necessary ones

In American English you *appeal* a decision, while Brits *appeal against* it. A matter of taste, perhaps, unless you are in the legal profession. But Americans also *protest a verdict*. In British English you have to protest *against* it, which preserves the useful distinction between protesting *against* a verdict and *protesting* (in the sense of asserting) *your innocence.*

CHAPTER 8

AYTMTB?

*Times change and our
vocabulary changes with them:
the hi-tech revolution*

The advent of social media, particularly the character-limitation of Twitter and the cumbersomeness of texting, has accelerated the development of language like nothing else in history. I'm not convinced that this is entirely a bad thing, and I have a distinguished American lexicographer on my side.

John McWhorter, in a TED talk about why – contrary to what many people maintain – texting isn't a scourge, makes the point that it isn't writing. It's a form of talking. He calls it 'fingered speech'. Just as spontaneous, everyday talking isn't like making a speech or giving a lecture, so texting isn't like formal writing. With a prepared speech or a literary work, you have the opportunity to pause, consider, reread and revise. In texting there is no question of this – you just dash it off the top of your head. You don't care about punctuation or the correct use of capital letters when you're talking; why should you in 'fingered speech'?

Giving an example of the new structure that characterizes the language of texting, McWhorter quotes a texted exchange between two young women that begins:

> A: I love the font you're using, btw.
> B: lol thanks gmail is being slow right now.
> A: lol, I know.

It's clear from this that *lol* doesn't mean literally *laugh out loud* (still less does it mean *lots of love*, as some much-ridiculed members of the older generation once suggested): it's simply an acknowledgement of what has gone before – McWhorter calls it a 'marker of empathy' or, more formally, a 'pragmatic particle'. We use this sort of thing in normal speech, too; I overheard a conversation in the street that went:

> A: I saw Richard yesterday.
> B: Oh, how's he doing?
> A: Yeah, he seems to be fine.

Similarly, I asked a friend how his wife was. 'Yeah, good,' he replied. 'Busy as ever . . .' and he went on to tell me what she was up to. Those *yeahs* don't mean 'yes': *yes* isn't an answer to a question beginning with *how*. They're friendly fillers that reinforce the statements following them. If they mean anything, it's 'Thank you for asking.' Another marker of empathy.

This isn't a scourge, says McWhorter, it's a linguistic miracle that means young people are effectively learning a second language – or at least a second dialect – alongside the 'real' one.

Nevertheless, you may feel that even empathy can go too far. I've heard, after someone had been in an accident:

A: I hope he isn't badly hurt.
B: Yes, no, he should be fine in a couple of days.

Is this usage insane? Or just the way it is? You choose.

Some new abbrevs

These young (and maybe not so young) texters and tweeters are also inventing any number of abbreviations: IMHO (in my humble opinion); ICYMI (in case you missed it); AYTMTB? (and you're telling me this because?); TMI (too much information); HTH (hope this helps); SFLR (sorry for late reply); AIBU (am I being unreasonable?); YOLO (you only live once – a way of inciting your correspondent to do something mildy outrageous); POS (parent over shoulder); and many, many more. Some of these are useful purely for the sake of brevity; one is a modern take on the age-old parent-teenager conflict; FFS avoids the necessity of swearing (the first and last initial stand for 'for' and 'sake'); and some have what Sherlock Holmes might have called 'other features of interest'.

What I particularly like about ICYMI is not the expression itself but the context in which it has come into being. Once upon a time, if you forgot to record something on television you simply missed it and there was nothing you could do about it until a repeat came along a year or so later; nowadays it'll be on the channel's catch-up service; somebody will have posted a link on social media; you'll find it on YouTube; or you can buy the boxed set within a few weeks. So having something pointed out to you 'in case you missed it' is of genuine value.

Despite the question mark that I choose to put at the end of it, *And you're telling me this because?* isn't really a question. It's an expression of complete lack of concern. In the cartoon *Peanuts*, Linus was once seen offering to throw a stick for Snoopy with the explanation, 'I, the human being, will throw the stick and you, the dog, will retrieve it.' Snoopy's dismissive response is 'I, the dog, could not be less interested.' AYTMTB is the same thing without the speech bubbles.

And my favourite of all these – one I find myself using more and more as I become more dogmatic in my old age – is IMHO. I like it not only because it comes in so handy, but because of a story a friend told from the days when he was a magazine editor dealing with a particularly pompous contributor. The contributor having ended a diatribe with this abbreviation, my friend was able to respond that the man had never had an HO in his L.

On the other hand, I have an aversion to JK. (I have an aversion to smiley emoticons, too.) There's something wrong when we have constantly to reassure our correspondents or our social media contacts that we are 'just kidding'. The fact that emoticons and emojis are as widely used as they are suggests that there are people out there who will disagree with me. I don't care. This is my book and that's what I think. EOD.

Acknowledgements

Whenever I write a book about language I am inundated with suggestions for points to include, from friends who have been annoyed by something they've heard on the radio or who simply come up with something witty. This time, I'd particularly like to thank Ann (for the mug), Carol, Cec, John C, Pom, Rebecca, Sam and Sue for their contributions, even if they didn't all realize I was writing down what they were saying.

Thanks also to Louise at Michael O'Mara for persuading me to write the book and to George for meticulous editing. Any mistakes, pomposities or prejudices that remain are entirely my own.

References

In writing this book I've been inspired, helped and amused in various ways by all the following:

Brandon, John G. *A Scream in Soho* (1940; British Library edition 2014)

Bryson, Bill *The Road to Little Dribbling: More notes from a small island* (Doubleday, 2015)

Dorren, Gaston *Lingo: A language spotter's guide to Europe* (Profile Books, 2014)

Gowers, Rebecca *Horrible Words* (Particular Books, 2016)

Greenbaum, Sidney, and Nelson, Gerald *An Introduction to English Grammar* (Pearson Education, third edition 2009)

Havel, Václav *Selected Plays 1963–83* (Faber & Faber, 1992)

Holmes, Oliver Wendell *The Autocrat of the Breakfast Table* (1858; Ward Lock UK edition 1910)

Mason, Mark *Mail Obsession: A journey round Britain by postcode* (Weidenfeld & Nicolson, 2015)

Melville, Alan *Quick Curtain* (1934; British Library edition 2015)

Poole, Steven *Unspeak* (Little, Brown, 2006)

Taggart, Caroline *Her Ladyship's Guide to the Queen's English* (National Trust, 2010)

Taggart, Caroline *New Words for Old* (Michael O'Mara Books, 2015)

Taggart, Caroline & J. A. Wines *My Grammar and I (or should that be 'Me'?)* (Michael O'Mara Books, 2008)

Webster, Jason *Or the Bull Kills You* (Chatto & Windus, 2011)

The discussion of *Finnegans Wake* (page 50) came my way thanks to a letter written to the *Guardian* by Philip Stogden, reprinted in *The Week*, 27 February 2016.

American Mensa's paragraph about acyrologia (page 120) is widely quoted on the internet, including at: http://accentuatewriters.com/viewthread.php?action=printable&fid=28&tid=19578

The report on Helen Clark's speech (pages 163–5) is by my friend Martin Mulligan: http://www.

commonwealthroundtable.co.uk/commonwealth/
orwells-duckspeak-commonwealth-discourse/

Bruce D. Price's article on Noun Overuse Phenomenon
(pages 168–9) can be found at: http://www.
verbatimmag.com/noun_overuse.html

John McWhorter's TED talk (pages 176–8) is at: http://
www.ted.com/playlists/228/how_language_
changes_over_time

Index

By *Sunday Times* bestselling author
Caroline Taggart

KICKING the BUCKET ~ at the ~ DROP of a HAT

The Meaning and Origins of Popular Expressions

Kicking the Bucket at the Drop of a Hat

978-1-78243-582-2

£7.99

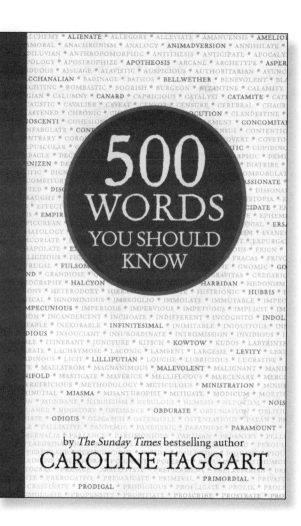

500 Words You Should Know

978-1-78243-294-4

£9.99

New Words for Old

978-1-78243-472-6

£9.99